AN END TO SILENCE

An End to Silence

DES WILSON

THE MERCIER PRESS
CORK and DUBLIN

The Mercier Press Limited
4 Bridge Street, Cork
24 Lower Abbey Street, Dublin 1

British Library Cataloguing in Publication Data

Wilson, Des
  An End To Silence.
  1. Christianity and politics 2. Church and State —
  Northern Ireland 3. Northern Ireland — Church history
  4. Northern Ireland — History — 1969
  I. Title
  941.60824   BR797.N67

ISBN 0 85342 756 9

Printed by Litho Press Co., Midleton, Co. Cork.

Contents

Author's Note

The terms 'Northern Ireland', 'the North of Ireland, 'the North' are used here because generally speaking people know that they refer to the territory in Ireland controlled by the British government. The terms are inaccurate because they give the impression that the territory is much larger than it really is, but a term like 'the British controlled six north-eastern counties of Ireland' which is an accurate description of the area discussed would be too unwieldy.

The term 'The Minority' to describe the Catholic population of this area is not used at all since it is not only politically dishonest but deliberately degrading.

Foreword

Northern Ireland is a corrupt state.

We need to understand what we mean by corruption: when our institutions, courts, parliament, police and churches fail to do what they were founded to do they are inefficient – but when they turn upside down and do the opposite of what they were intended to do they are corrupt; courts which dispense injustice, parliaments which work for the advantage of only a section of the people, police who attack rather than defend, churches which contribute not to human dignity but to human pain.

Not everyone will accept such a definition of corruption, preferring to confine it to sexual misbehaviour or putting a hand in the till, but the wider definition is useful for political analysis, and in any case includes these two in a wider context of oppressions which should be equally unacceptable.

To say the state is corrupt is not necessarily to blame the people; politicians and churchmen there have consistently failed to create an idealism which would match that of the people as a whole. The corruption is all the more tragic because Northern Ireland is one part of an experiment in creating a Christian state. What should a Christian state be like? Northern Ireland is the Protestant version, the Republic of Ireland is the Catholic version.

This experiment in creating ideal Christian states according to Catholic and Protestant principles has been a sad and costly failure; evidence, if we need it, that confessional states including Christian ones can cause more pain than they are worth.

Because Britain wanted to hold on to the six north-eastern counties of Ireland for economic and military reasons, churchmen found themselves in an unique position – they were able to help create Christian states according to their own principles, ideals and beliefs. They did it, and so the two states in Ireland today are the result not of Christian failure but of Christian success; they did nearly everything they set out to do.

But now in the North of Ireland lawyers admit that the courts condemn the innocent, churchmen admit that more and more Christians are finding their way out of churches rather than unbelievers into them, torture has been used, is being used, to extract confessions of guilt while many citizens believe that if they call it 'ill-treatment' it ceases to be wrong; business and political affairs are inspired by principles no different from principles elsewhere, and so far from leading the flock into quiet pastures, religious shepherds are often in the first rank of those who fill their lives with turmoil.

In the Republic there has been a continuing struggle for power between politicians and clergy. In 1949 when I was ordained I remember a queue a hundred yards long, headed by the president of Ireland, waiting to kiss the cardinal's ring. Since that time the scene has changed. The clergy have been losing the battle for supremacy and now it is becoming more and more possible for politicians to challenge some of the beliefs most insistently taught by clergy and not suffer politically for it. The power struggle which is going on is fluid, and normal in this or any other Christian society. Whether the political, economic or social life in the Republic is good or bad, there are many people who complain about it bitterly: their complaint is not about there being too much principle in it, it is about the lack of it.

In the Christian state it is almost inevitable that churchmen will be used by politicians and politicians by churchmen for religious and political reasons. This has its own penalties. One of the prime ministers of Northern Ireland, Lord Brookeborough, spent all his political life defending the Protestant heritage which he said he shared and so in this defence politicians and churchmen were united. When he retired from politics, however, Brookeborough made it known that he was really an agnostic. But the price was paid in full – today the two largest political parties in the North, the Official Unionist Party and the Democratic Unionist Party, are dominated by Christian clergymen.

Although Christians said that it is the truth that sets us free they had to hide the reality of what they were doing. Not only did some of them have to pretend to a depth of faith which they did not have but what was even more despicable, they had to pretend to be bigots when in fact they were not. Brian Faulkner, it can be argued, belonged to the second of these categories. Hiding things was necessary at all levels. Politicians in Westminster invented the 'gentlemen's agreement' not to talk about Northern Ireland; churchmen in Northern Ireland who talked about the duties of the rich – which Christian theology was concerned about – carefully avoided mention of the rights of poor people to defend themselves if the rich did not carry out their duties – which Christian theology was also concerned about. When poor Catholics and poor Protestants took matters into their own hands from time to time and filled the streets with their cries and their missiles there were always politicians and preachers who vied with each other to inflame them with sectarian fear and distrust which their common hunger had for the moment caused them to forget. It was more important that they be persuaded to forget their common interests and their need to defend them together.

Christians in Ireland, then, whose attention had been directed often towards the persecutions in Russia, Mexico or Spain, failed to notice that the oppressions they had created for themselves were remarkably similar to those they complained about when they happened somewhere else. But the truth cannot be hidden for ever. The Christians as a body were rich, influential. Why then could their resources and international connections not be used to help relieve poverty at home and heal the differences between the people in the Christian states themselves?

From the mid-1950s until the present time there came some awakening of consciences in Northern Ireland but while this was happening it became clear that what we were dealing with was not after all the wrong people in powerful positions but powerful positions so constructed that only wrong could be the result of them. Institutional violence was a fact of life in Ireland too.

The institutions in the states spoke to each other, clung to each other, shared methods, aims and standards. The state, the churches and the army began to be seen as having common interests. A Protestant clergyman in the North calling for support of the forces of law and order, a cardinal in the South inspecting a military guard of honour evoked thoughts of similar and more sinister connections abroad. When Pope John Paul II on his visit to Ireland (1979) was carried in an Irish army helicopter and had lunch with the Minister for Defence – not, for example, the minister responsible for social welfare – nobody seemed to notice. Perhaps Irish people had become accustomed to such connections. There was no suggestion that delicacy if not policy

should dictate that churchmen and army men keep their distance
from each other.

Dissent in any of the institutions is not easy, it is less easy than,
for example, leading a disorderly life within the institutions. One
can lead a disorderly life within our institutions – army,
government, church – to a quite surprising extent and still survive
as a serving officer. But if one opposes the policies of these
institutions one can very quickly be marginalised, moved aside in
the church or army, expelled from the party. It is normal.

My own experience of being marginalised, although the most
bitterly resented experience of my life, involved little more than
being forbidden the use of church buildings and resources, with
the consequent and intended loss of reputation this action brings
with it. For those in Northern Ireland who opposed the state it
was much harder than that. Many of them had to contend with
prison, torture or even death. An interesting aspect of our
institutions is the similarity in methods used or approved of:
marginalisation, destruction of reputation, withdrawal of
resources, imprisonment, death. The death penalty has been
called for more frequently and more insistently in Northern
Ireland by Christian clergymen than by any other professional
group.

It has been said that the situation in the North of Ireland is
very complex. So it is, and therefore the reasons, motivations and
interpretations of fact which influence people are confusing. The
more confusing the situation the more single-minded a person
must be in trying to understand it. One can understand only a bit
of it at a time. But as one studies this piece of the scene or that a
pattern begins to emerge.

The pattern is very similar to what we see in political situations
in other countries. The citizens of Northern Ireland are not
victims of some weird disaster, some unaccountable going wrong
of what should have gone right. They are victims of decisions and
choices carefully made by their religious and political leaders.
These leaders did not fail. They succeeded. There lies the tragedy
of the place.

Dean Swift wrote: 'We have just enough religion to make us
hate but not enough to make us love one another.' Perhaps,
though, the trouble is not that people do not have enough religion,
they are deeply religious, like all people, but rather that in our

condition it is politically and ecclesiastically dangerous to express it.

It must be difficult to solve problems humanely when so much of the resources of our political, cultural and religious institutions are also occupied helping to create or prolong them.

1

A Personal View

In 1935 when I was growing up in Belfast my father brought me down town to show me the barricades in the streets separating Catholics at one end from Protestants at the other. I accepted as a fact of life that for some reason I did not understand Catholics and Protestants fight each other.

What I did not know until much later was that just three years before, Catholics and Protestants from those same districts were desperately trying to reach out to each other, to march together in the streets against poverty, unemployment and injustice. In 1932 there was some hope that they would stand together in the streets and sometimes they did; by 1935 they had retreated to their homes again in the fear that they would be burned out in the sectarian fury once again successfully aroused among themselves and their neighbours. Why did it happen?

In the 1960s we were asking the same question for much the same reasons. About the beginning of the 1960s a movement was going on in the North of Ireland of a kind most of us had never experienced before. People of very different religious and political views were meeting, exchanging views and exchanging courtesies. Unionists were invited to speak to Nationalists and people of different religious and political views shared platforms and seminars. The excitement at the time for those who were close to that movement was very great. There was a great simplicity and naïvety in much of it.

I was invited some time during that period to speak to a group called the Republican Felons Club. The only useful thing I could talk about was the changes coming about in the churches. There are changes coming, the members said, so we want to talk about how we can help these changes to happen. At the end of the meeting I asked who was coming to the next discussion. They named a prominent Unionist politician. That was a symbol of the times, a Unionist politician invited to a club on the Falls Road every one of whose members had suffered imprisonment and other hardships because they were Republicans. It was a time for rethinking, for losing some of the fear we had been brought up with, for planning a new kind of religious and political life.

By August 1969 the houses were burning once again. Past the door of the Republican Felons Club, which had extended that hand of friendship a few years before, something like 8,000 refugees were streaming for safety into other people's already over-crowded homes and improvised reception centres.

In the 1930s the period between hope and despair had been about three years; in the 1960s it was about ten.

That pattern has always been the same; people coming together, mingling in the streets, inter-marrying, working together if they were allowed to, then inevitably agitation from preachers and politicians leading to street violence, house-burning and bloodshed.

It was not something that happened accidentally or because the people were violent or peculiar, it was a carefully contrived political process which we gradually came to recognise as a periodic redistribution of population and property by pogrom. People had to be driven into political and religious ghettos where the effect of their vote would be controllable; property, especially lucrative public houses, came under new management. In the upheavals from 1969 onwards in Northern Ireland over 600 public houses were attacked as the population and property adjustments were made by gunfire and house-burning. Of these many were reopened under new management, the religious affiliation of the new management being, of course, different from that of the old one.

The ploy was not new. A Church of Ireland clergyman who ministered in East Belfast in the 1920s has written about a severe crusade against alcohol which took place in his district during that time. Riots broke out and the spirit grocers, who sold alcohol and groceries side by side, were among the first to come under attack. It was more or less what the preacher expected. But what surprised and shocked him was the speed with which licensed premises were reopened under new management which in many cases consisted of members of his own parish. Redistribution of population and property by pogrom for electoral and financial reasons – and not purely religious conflict – was the reality of the situation.

Naturally, many of us who lived in Belfast wanted to change all that. We were naïve and innocent. We believed it would be possible to obtain good government within the British connection. If we could settle whatever differences there were between Catholics and Protestants the way would be open for good government. We had always been led to believe that we as Catholics and Protestants were the problem; it was only after many years of fruitless attempts at peace-making and reconciliation that we were forced to recognise that we were in fact the victims of a problem which had been carefully created for us by the British government.

The pattern was fixed then. Whatever we tried to do, and as far as one could see, useful attempts at reconciliation would inevitably be followed by agitation and religious strife stirred up by political and religious *agents provocateurs* and our efforts would be destroyed. The redistribution of property and population by pogrom which occurred on average every ten years or so was a necessary part of the system of British government in Northern Ireland. Without it the people would do as they had always done, reach out to each other and begin to find common ground for agreement. The primary evil was not, it then appeared, antagonism between Protestants and Catholics as such. It was the existence of a regime for which the end of conflict and pogrom would spell the end of the regime.

This, however, was a conclusion one reached only reluctantly, not, in fact, until the rise of Paisley in the 1960s, the civil rights marches at the end of the decade and what has happened ever since. Coming as I did from a conservative background in which we believed in the essential goodness of our various institutions it was a difficult position at which to arrive. It had to be worked out painfully at every step of the way. When we were growing up we realised, of course, that as Catholics we had no chance of ever taking part in the government of our own country. Our chances of progressing in professions and jobs, or even of getting into many of them, were very limited. The secret societies seemed more efficient and sinister the older we grew and the more we experienced the impossibility of reaching any rational agreement with the British regime. We were excluded from much of the political, economic and social life of the area we lived in not only because it was presumed we would vote against the government but because no matter how we might vote we were still Catholics. Protestants who were Socialists or Nationalists were likely to be treated in much the same way, but whereas they could repent and join the ruling Unionist Party – as the one time Socialist Harry Midgley did in 1944, Catholics who wanted to do everything possible to take part in government were forbidden membership of the Unionist Party. The Alliance Party in Northern Ireland founded in 1970 was created to give a political home to Catholic Unionists who otherwise would have no party in which to be involved.

Those of us who did not belong to the ruling party were powerless. Our elected representatives could not have any real influence on what went on in parliament or council chamber; they had to be content with small deals which could be done in the corridors with Unionists who were decent enough to patronise them. T. J. Campbell was one of the Nationalists who worked the system in this degrading way. He wrote about it afterwards in *Fifty Years of Ulster*, and was probably the first to point out that the only law which Nationalists were able to influence was one for the protection of wild birds. They could not influence laws for the protection of their own people. As a rule even their amendments were refused.

What we were slowest of all to understand was that even if the British government were willing to help create a democracy in all Ireland for the first time in its history it would probably be unable to do so. The 1916 Rebellion was resented and feared because it could well hasten the break up of the British Empire. Might the loss of Northern Ireland hasten the break up of the United Kingdom?

The problems revealed during the past twenty years as the situation in Northern Ireland developed were much more complicated and difficult than people could ever have imagined when they began their long journey towards good government in the 1960s. We were slow to accept that if the British government were to suffer a constitutional crisis as a result of a just settlement in Ireland that was their problem, not ours. It took a long time for us to overcome our inbred respect for the British government sufficiently to admit that if they had problems they should be forced to solve them at their own, and not at our, expense.

Those who demanded radical political change were marginalised not only politically, economically and socially but even by the use of words. The British government implied that to oppose their regime was to be a terrorist or a friend of terrorists. The Irish government accepted that political and moral judgement, while many churchmen made the words 'Republican' or 'Socialist' unrespectable too. A citizen is nearly always afraid to be dubbed what governments and powerful people deem unrespectable. The answer to this problem is for citizens not to accept the definitions offered by governments and refuse to accept either republicans or socialists, but to insist upon discussing such words openly so as to discover how their respectability compares with that of others, monarchism or capitalism, for example.

The concept of terrorism has also to be discussed and assessed. Professor Alfred McClung Lee has done this in the United States (*Terrorism in Northern Ireland*, 1983). In Ireland we have hardly yet dared to do so.

We have to be clear about what the real issues are. We are attempting to create a modern democracy in Ireland. It has to be a democracy which, being modern and suited to the needs and genius of the Irish people, will be different, in some respects, from that of the British state. The reasons why Irish people assert their right to do this are based upon modern reasonable, democratic principles. The reasons why the British oppose it are based upon what they see as their own economic and military needs, and possibly also because to create a democracy in Ireland would throw open to question the nature of democracy in Britain. International terrorism is not what the Northern Ireland conflict is about and the sooner we insist upon a rational discussion of that term the better. Are we using it as a means of analysing political problems in Ireland or simply as a term of abuse? Unless we give the term 'international terrorism' an extraordinary meaning we shall in all probability find that it has nothing to do with Ireland and Ireland has nothing to do with it. The edifice of propaganda which has been built upon the term by politicians and churchmen can be a nuisance but it is remediable.

As a Christian I share the belief of Christians that each person is created by God, renewed by Christ and inspired by the Holy Spirit. Therefore, each person is entitled – by God, not by us, not even by voters – to be heard and respected. To exclude forty per cent of the people of any country from an effective part in their own government is immoral as well as politically wrong. This situation must be changed. But in order to change it we have only a few means at our disposal, in contrast to governments, which have many. We must be able to choose adequate means – not just means acceptable to the regime – by which we shall make political progress. We must be free to meet whomever we wish to meet, not just people approved by the regime, to discuss whatever we wish to talk about. We must be free to communicate with our fellow citizens no matter who they are. A system which keeps people separate from each other for political or religious reasons cannot be defended and must be dissolved. If we wish to do so then we are entitled by our own dignity to meet everyone including members of militant and military groups. As a citizen I shall meet whom I wish to meet.

During the past fifteen years my friends have included men and women who were members of political groups, some of them approving the use of arms against the government or for maintaining the political status quo in the North. So far from making any apology for this I am very glad of it. It helped me to understand that governments not only try to prevent us meeting evil people, they also try to prevent us meeting those whom they want us to believe are evil, whether they are evil or not. Among our Protestant friends there were some who, I am convinced, risked their lives to bring Catholics and Protestants, Republicans and Loyalists together. They were members of militant and perhaps military organisations. If any churchman took the same risks I would give him the same respect. Friends among the Republican groups were always willing to meet and discuss with the same end in view. No government is going to tell me how I should have behaved towards Sammy Smyth who was supposed to be involved with the UDA, or John McKeague (Red Hand Commandos) who in the last two years of his life talked long and earnestly about how we could help all our people together, or Ronnie Bunting the Republican Socialist, or Máire Drumm of Sinn Féin. I knew how to behave towards them because they were my friends. All of them were assassinated. There were others, but I mention these especially because all of them were people whom by government order I was supposed to hate or avoid.

As time passed it seemed less reasonable to condemn those who took up arms against the government or against their fellow-citizens without discussing why they did it and whether they saw any alternative open to them. We had said, in agreement with the British and Irish governments, that those who took up arms against the British regime in Northern Ireland were terrorists and acting immorally. What they were doing showed that they were immoral. What we should have been saying was: 'Look, here are good people, Protestants, Catholics, men and women of character some of whom have gone to the extreme of taking up arms – surely some terrible reason must have driven people of that quality to do it?'

No one will claim that all political activists are morally good; it is unjust to claim that they are all bad – unjust and too easy.

The trouble with thinking this way is that it goes against government policy. It also means asking people to stop locking away their fellow citizens in the darkness of high security prisons and instead to bring out into the light of day the reasons which make them do as they do.

2

British Institutions of Government

The Northern Ireland situation is represented as a great British democracy – one of the greatest in the world – standing at great cost to itself between undemocratic warring factions there.

But the British system of government cannot properly be called a modern democracy. The assumption which Irish people make that British political institutions are superior to their own, or even that they are equally acceptable, is false.

For example, no modern democrat is likely to accept a hereditary monarchy irrevocably attached to a single rich and powerful family, the most militarist in the European Community. We read with dismay about military juntas in other countries but the existence in Britain of an exceptionally rich royal family whose members are highly placed in the armed forces never excites even a comment. That a monarch can be at one and the same time head of armed forces, head of state and head of a state church may seem little more than a quaint ritualistic survival of past glory, but since the powers of the monarch within the British system are great, ill-defined and not controlled by a written constitution, what we are dealing with in Britain is not, in this particular case, a modern democracy so much as a modified, archaic and still powerful monarchical system of government. If we were to read of the wife of some dictator in a dynastic South American dictatorship acting in all these capacities we would murmur about the nature of the regime. When it happens in Britain we seem to have an inbuilt desire to believe somehow it must be all right. The queen mother as admiral of the fleet or the husband of the queen as the head of the armed forces contrasts with the provisions of the Irish (1937) Constitution which vests supreme command of the armed forces in a president elected by the people, not in a rich family whose powers pass on from mother and father to sons and daughters whether people approve of them   or not.

The upper house in the British parliamentary system is also undemocratic. There is no other nation in the European Community which allows an upper house that is unelected and consists largely of rich landowners to have any effective say in the making of their laws. Under the Irish Constitution such an institution is impossible. The desire to portray the British system of government as superior and the Irish as inferior has prevented any discussion of the nature of the British political system. That is a pity, and until there is such a realistic discussion we can never fully understand the real meaning of the conflict in the North.

The upper house of the British parliamentary system consists of about one thousand lords, most of whom have their titles and wealth by hereditary succession. Comparatively few members are 'life peers', that is, men and women who are not aristocrats but are placed in the House of Lords to give it a more democratic appearance and to introduce an element of the popular voice. The life peers are chosen by the prime minister and other party leaders and created by the monarch and so are a strictly controlled group in quality and numbers. In some cases life peers have been created who had already been rejected by the vote of the people. Lord Fitt, for example, was made a life peer in 1983 having been rejected by the voters of West Belfast that same year.

It is argued that the House of Lords has little power. If it has any power at all over the making of laws then by this much its influence in the British system is undemocratic. As I have already said, there is no other nation in the European Community which allows a house of rich landowners and state-appointed churchmen to have an almost final say in the passing of its laws; laws have to be approved by the unelected lords and final approval must be given by the hereditary monarch.

People in Ireland have consistently refused to acknowledge the archaic and undemocratic nature of this kind of government. This may be because they wish to preserve the myth of the superiority of British institutions. Perhaps there is somewhere in the soul of Irish people a deep longing and respect for aristocrats. The French dragged them on the tumbrils and the Irish burned their houses, but the evidence is that they loved them all the same.

Neither the French nor the Irish, however, loved them so much as to allow them to prevent, hold up or amend the laws which the people had elected their parliament to make. Only the British do that. It is hardly likely that modern democrats will agree with the system. It is hardly likely either that modern democrats will reconcile themselves to a system in which when a citizen has been through every court in the land his case will then be heard not by elected people of his own choice, not by his equals, not by lawyers chosen because of their exceptional legal wisdom only, but by members of the House of Lords who were elected by nobody and may be just as good or as inept as any other lawyers in the land.

Irish people may remember in this connection that on one occasion (1893) it was not the British people who prevented home rule for Ireland, not the British cabinet, not even the British Commons elected by the people; it was the unelected House of Lords.

No modern democracy would willingly tolerate a state church. In Britain there is a state church whose bishops are appointed by the monarch on the advice of the prime minister of the day. One or both could be agnostics but nevertheless they appoint the Christian bishops of the state (Anglican) church. In return twenty-six of the state-appointed bishops are allowed to sit and to vote in the House of Lords. In Ireland there is no state church. The recognition given to the Catholic church in the 1937 Constitution – that it was the guardian of the faith of the majority of Irish citizens – was considered by the people as going much too far and deleted. When we discuss the sectarian nature of the Irish state as against the widely assumed pluralist nature of the British state, such things are never mentioned.

Why they are not mentioned one can only guess. Certainly it is extraordinary that in a discussion of pluralism and sectarianism the existence in Britain of state-appointed churchmen who influence the making of laws is not considered important enough to talk about. Many Irish people are unhappy with their own Constitution and wish it changed because they believe it is not democratic enough. It cannot be wondered at that people in the North who have been for so long ruled by a British system which is not only undemocratic but virtually unchangeable are unwilling to be ruled by it any more. They are too mature to be ruled by archaisms. The last serious effort made by the major British political parties to bring about some changes, not radical changes, in their House of Lords was in 1968. The attempt failed. What the British political parties were trying to do at that time was to move their upper house in the direction of becoming a more democratic assembly, in other words, in the direction which Irish people had already moved more than thirty years previously.

It becomes more and more offensive to Irish democrats to be told that they, and not the British, are the opponents of democracy.

A study of the British system reveals that it is archaic, insufficiently developed for modern needs, and in some respects dangerous not only to other nations but to the British themselves. British political writers do not know the full extent or the precise nature of the powers which the monarch has in her Privy Council. The Privy Council consisting of some three hundred people chosen by the monarch herself can make decisions which are, as the word 'privy' denotes, secret. Members of the Privy Council take an oath of secrecy about their discussions. No modern democracy, including the Irish, would tolerate this kind of situation for a moment longer than it was forced to. The British accept it and are powerless to change it. The absence of a written constitution together with the power of monarchy, aristocracy and other institutions in the state cripple all efforts to make substantial change.

It is not, of course, some quirk of the British character that makes such archaisms and anomalies – or undemocratic procedures – possible. During the Second World War the nations of Europe suffered enormously, materially, spiritually and politically. Not only were their cities destroyed, in some cases their political structures were destroyed as well. After the war their political systems had to be reconstructed. In Germany, France and Italy for example, the economy, social life and political systems had to be restructured.

Naturally a number of these European countries moved, broadly speaking, in the direction which the needs of a modern democracy seemed to require, a reduction of monarchical or personal powers and an increase in the powers of elected parliaments. The powers taken on by De Gaulle were at least not hereditary but had to be approved by the people. It was a dangerous, often frustrating, and in many ways a disappointing process. But changes had to be made and were made.

In Britain it was different. There was no need to restructure the political system because it had survived intact. With some adjustments the old system could continue. The result is that there is today in Britain the most undeveloped political system in the European Community, with a powerful monarchy, an unelected parliamentary upper house of rich landowners, privy council, leadership of church and armed forces vested in one rich and powerful family and so on. The British system found itself in the post war years stuck in its own anachronisms and unable to change. The power of the monarchy, aristocracy and other vested interests was too great to be forced to change.

The meaning of this for Irish democrats is easy to see. When they look to Britain for the creation of a modern democracy in Ireland they have to remember the saying, 'Ye canna' tak' the breeks aff a Highlander', or more elegantly, *Nemo dat quod non habet*, you cannot give what you haven't got. If the British have not a modern democracy in their own country it is impossible to give one to the Irish.

We recognise their difficulties. If the forms of government which Irish democrats want for their own country were conceded in the North it would in all probability cause a constitutional crisis in Britain. It would raise too many questions about the real nature of democracy there and even about the nature of the British state.

It is not some quirk of the British character that makes the British government act as it does in Ireland. Given the kind of government it is it could hardly do otherwise. No nation can afford to act abroad in a way that will cause constitutional difficulties and possibly a constitutional crisis at home.

How a powerful nation behaves towards an emerging democracy is decided not by the needs of the new democracy but by its own needs. The attitude of the United States to Nicaragua, of the Soviet Union to Poland, of Britain to Ireland, has little to do with the needs of the smaller countries which wish to develop politically in their own way. It has everything to do with the needs of the larger blocs who are determined not to develop any further except territorially and commercially. In the Irish situation democrats have to say to the British government, 'Very well, do what you like in your own country but do not impose archaic and undemocratic forms of government on us; our standards of democracy are already higher. We have no wish to allow them to remain even as they are, let alone lower them.'

So far from being a great democracy standing between the

opponents of democracy in Ireland the British regime is the greatest obstacle to the development of democracy that we have. Its potential to inhibit the creation of a modern democracy in Ireland must, therefore, be dissolved. Irish people must stop apologising for themselves or for the Constitution they created when they were free to do so in the 1920s and 1930s. These constitutions with all their faults were far ahead of anything the British had ever conceived of as being a democratic system of government.

We can honourably say to the British government, 'Either you make your system a modern democracy and in that case you will have some reason for asking us to stay with you or if you cannot do this then you must get out of our country.' Any modern democrat will understand our position, but we have to explain it in these terms.

We speak of the 'British' government but what we are actually dealing with is an *English* government. Most of the members of the British cabinet are elected for English constituencies. There is a Secretary of State for Scotland, one for Wales and one for Northern Ireland, but while they have powers which exceed anyone else's in these areas, in the cabinet they have practically no power at all. The Secretary for Northern Ireland is not even Irish. The important posts in cabinet are held by members elected by English people for English constituencies. If there were, let us say, power-sharing within the British cabinet we should expect, on the basis of population, that a number of seats in cabinet would go to members from Scottish, Welsh and Northern Ireland constituencies, perhaps four or five in all. This, however, does not happen. The cabinet is British in the sense that it claims power over England, Scotland, Wales and part of Ireland. It is English in that it does not have built-in power-sharing with representatives from Scotland, Wales and Ireland. Finance, defence and other important posts are held by members from English constituencies. This need not always be so, of course. It depends upon the prime minister; but there is no built-in right to power-sharing within the system.

If then this English government were to give to the people in the North of Ireland a form of government which included inbuilt rights of power-sharing for Nationalist and Republican, Unionist and Loyalist, Catholic and Protestant, it would be giving to the

North of Ireland a system more democratic than that available to the people of Scotland and Wales, who could reasonably say, 'If you insist on power-sharing in one part of the United Kingdom we insist upon it in another; we require seats as of right for the Scots and Welsh in cabinet.'

This, of course, cannot be conceded. The English cabinet must remain entirely or predominantly English. Power-sharing in Britain is out. One suspects, then, that there were other and more compelling reasons for the failure of the power-sharing Executive in the North of Ireland in 1974 than the Loyalist workers' strike.

The British government has successfully portrayed Irish people as dreamers, unfitted to create democracy, living in and off the past. The image of starry-eyed idealists, of soft spoken conmen and conwomen, of people who are bigots, and even if silent bigots all the more dangerous for that, has been carefully fostered in Ireland and abroad. In foreign countries British propaganda about Ireland has been accepted almost without question. It is only in recent years that commentators in France, Italy, Germany, the United States and Britain itself have become aware that in Ireland the situation is not as British Information Services describe it. The thrust of British propaganda abroad had been to portray Irish people as, at worst, ignorant, violent and stupid, at best, unpractical idealists. A very large amount of money is spent by the British government on propaganda of this kind, an amount which has increased sharply in recent years as British propaganda explanations have been increasingly questioned abroad. The printed propaganda of the government shows a strange mixture of sophistication and naïvete. The standard of production of information sheets etc., which flood the American universities, church magazines and newspapers is high; the quality of argument is low. It would seem that having had a free hand for so long British propagandists have not had to exert themselves. In recent years they have had to exert themselves more as the case for British withdrawal from Ireland has been seen to be both democratic and rational. If it had not been for the ready co-operation of successive Irish governments British propaganda abroad would probably have been a more difficult task. As it was, the British government had little if any official opposition.

I had a conversation some years ago (1976) in Rome with the Irish Ambassador to the Vatican there. He told me that every time

a major political event occurred in Ireland the British
representative in the Vatican went to the Vatican Secretariate of
State with all speed to give the official British version. Any other
representative would need to be very fleet of foot to get there first.
Some time later I received a similar story from Archbishop Bruno
Heim. Every time a major political event occurred in Ireland he
was sure of a speedy visit from a British official to tell him the
British version. Bruno Heim was the Vatican's London based
diplomatic representative in Britain.

The democratic claims to Irish sovereignty, then, were heard
at the Vatican only in the face of very strong British counter-
arguments.

Elsewhere, when demands for changes in Ireland were made
they were often made not in terms of a modern, rational,
democratic argument but in terms of a kind of low-grade stage
Irish blather of the sort seen and heard in profusion during John
Kennedy's visit to Ireland, and worse, Ronald Reagan's; and in
the occasional political messages of Mr O'Neill, Mr Carey, the
Kennedys and Mr Moynihan in the United States – a deliberate
rejection of reason in favour of rhetoric.

How vulnerable the British message is, however, can be seen
from time to time. Hurried interventions by British diplomatic
officials abroad to prevent or inhibit conferences about Ireland,
their inability to confront rational political argument in public
debate, and actions like that of the BBC in August 1985 in banning
the televising of a programme containing an interview with Martin
McGuinness, a Sinn Féin member from Derry.

For the British government there is more at stake than refusing
to allow the British public to hear Martin McGuinness as a
member of an Irish political party. The problem with showing a
member of Sinn Féin is that the image already presented to the
British public of irrational thugs, criminals who kill and destroy
because that is all they want to do, must be preserved. To have
anyone appear before the public who would give the appearance
of being sane, and to have political reasons for what he encourages
people to do, would be to destroy the image carefully built up
over the years of the Irish in general as irrational and of Republicans in particular, as criminals. One aspect of the political reality
of Ireland may be allowed to come through, bombings or Paisley
speeches for example, another is filtered out. The Irish govern-

ment in order to create and preserve the same image censors radio and television with even greater consistency and force.

When some such act of censorship occurs in the BBC there is a shocked reaction because it is assumed, indeed proclaimed, in Ireland that the BBC is notable for its impartiality and fairness. If we were to ask who caused us to believe this we would probably have to admit that the BBC did so itself by constantly repeating the theme that the BBC is the fairest, most balanced broadcasting corporation in the world. It never was, and when we have looked critically at other British institutions and seen their true nature it is less difficult to understand the true nature of the BBC. One could say it sardonically, 'Of course the BBC is fair to everyone. Doesn't the British monarch appoint the governors of the BBC to make sure it will be?'

In Ireland the situation is different. The RTE Authority is appointed by the government, which itself is elected by the people. All Irish people are not by any means satisfied that RTE is as efficient or as rational as they would wish. Indeed no one would say it is politically independent, but at least they do not have to accept a system where the governors of a broadcasting authority are appointed by a monarch who is appointed by nobody. The Irish broadcasting system is curable, the BBC is not, for the same reasons that the House of Lords is not. In Northern Ireland the political nature of the BBC is illustrated by the fact that Lady Faulkner, wife of the late Brian Faulkner, was for years a governor of the BBC in Northern Ireland and for some time chairperson of the board. The governing body of the BBC reflects not the decisions and needs of the people as a whole but those of very powerful people who can, if they wish, govern broadcasting with their own interests in mind. If the BBC acts censoriously we should not be surprised. What should surprise us is the fact that no one in Ireland questions the nature of the BBC any more than they question the nature of the British political system. It is a highly politicised broadcasting company which has never been either impartial or independent. Perhaps if they did they might decide that the system is a just one or that it works well. They might decide, on the other hand, that it is both undemocratic and dangerous.

One can reasonably argue that it would be possible for vested interests in Britain, monarchy, aristocracy, army, state church acting together to take over power in Britain without breaking a single constitutional law. British commentators say they will never do this because there exist certain 'gentlemen's agreements' by which everyone understands that such things will not be done! This bizarre defence of the system is the response which will be given to an Irish, American or French democrat who insists that a modern democracy requires a written constitution in order to impose curbs on powerful groups within a state. The fact that the hereditary monarch in Britain appoints bishops, prime ministers, governors of the BBC, judges, has some political importance, but in our discussions about the nature of our problem with Britain we act as though it has none.

How powerful, then, are the British institutions to thwart our wishes? How powerful are they to thwart even the wishes of their own people, parliament or even government? Two events which occurred in Ireland give some indication of how even the will of parliament or cabinet in Britain may not be paramount.

The first was the so-called Curragh mutiny in 1914 when British troops in Ireland refused to make themselves available to enforce a political arrangement on Loyalists in the North. It is an event which is well known and need not be recounted here.

The other event took place in Northern Ireland in 1974. The British and Irish governments, together with the Alliance Party, the SDLP and some Unionists, made an agreement that a power-sharing executive should be set up in Northern Ireland. A strike was called by Loyalists and following this the power-sharing executive collapsed. During the strike those of us who lived in Northern Ireland could see what was going on and the difference between real happenings and official explanations.

Loyalists lined the streets and prevented traffic from flowing. They were armed with cudgels. The strikers caused a run down of electricity supplies. The British army was on the streets also, with its guns pointed not towards the Loyalist strikers but towards the Nationalist districts which the Loyalists were isolating. The Unionists had been deprived of their government at Stormont, the B-Specials, an armed police force and other things as well and in every case the British army was strong enough to help enforce what had been decided in these matters by its own government. But when the power-sharing executive was about to fall they said they had not the power to confront the Loyalists or the manpower to run the electricity stations. They did have the ability to manage the power stations; and the Loyalists were insufficiently armed, not well organised, and heavily infiltrated by police and military. Their capacity for any kind of street resistance was severely limited. The fact was not that the army was incapable of enforcing the government's decision on the Loyalists, it was that once again it had made itself unavailable to carry out the wishes of its own government. The explanation given officially was that Loyalists – who had not been strong enough to prevent the destruction of their own government in 1972 – were strong enough now in 1974 to thwart the British government, the Irish government and the combined influence of the SDLP, the Alliance Party and a section of the Unionist Party.

One may suspect that the Bloody Sunday episode in Derry was another instance of a refusal by one British institution, the army, to be at the service of another, even its own government, if what was required was not agreeable to it. At a conference in Oxford we had been told that the British government had no longer any reason for staying in Ireland, that neither strategy nor economics needed it, that the morale of the troops was low – what was needed was an honourable way out. Returning home from that conference we were met by people at Belfast airport who told us what had happened in Derry that afternoon. That was Bloody Sunday, 1972. Whatever the British Department of Defence might say, the British army would do what it pleased.

When Irish democrats say that if there is to be an armed force in the North during a period of negotiation it must not be the British army, this is not simply because the army has proved brutal and unacceptable. It is because we know from experience that if the British government were to create even a moderately just solution for Northern Ireland their own army would probably be unwilling to help to enforce it, especially if it appeared that such a solution would cause a constitutional crisis in Britain.

Until we face the realities of our own and the British situation we shall never be able to create an 'initiative' for the North of Ireland which will produce anything of value. We need to know the reality of the forces which would oppose or destroy a rational solution. The mere possibility, however, that Unionists, or any sector of the British political system, would oppose it should not make us afraid to create whatever rational initiative we can. The

British government has received a remarkably tolerant acceptance
of its 'initiatives' from Irish people. Since 1969, however, Irish
people themselves have suggested various possibilities for the
future and almost all such suggestions have been severely
criticised and rejected: a united Ireland, a federated Ireland of
two states, a federated Ireland of four states, an independent
Northern Ireland (or Ulster), integration of Northern Ireland
with England, Scotland and Wales, a return of the pre-1972
Stormont system. There is no need to discuss the merits of these
suggestions here. Two points only need by made.

One is that suggestions coming from any Irish source, including
Loyalists, have met with much more severe criticism in Ireland
than suggestions coming from the British government.

The other is that in all our discussions about initiatives not one
of these suggestions was on the table for discussion. The only
possibility on the table for discussion was that proposed by the
British government itself – and by nobody else – namely, overall
control from Westminster, with compulsory power-sharing built
into a local Northern Ireland administration.

That is to say, the British government told the people in
Northern Ireland that it wanted them to sit down together and
work out what their future should be. However, when they were
asked, 'Can we discuss a united Ireland?' the answer was, 'No.'
'A federated Ireland?' 'No.' 'An independent Ulster?' 'No.'
'Integration, return of the old Stormont regime?' 'No.' 'What then
can we discuss?'

We could discuss the one solution proposed by the British
government and no one else, a proposal which not only was not
put forward by people in the North but had been rejected by most
of them – enforced power-sharing in an internal solution.

Those living outside Northern Ireland may wonder why
politicians in the North are unwilling to discuss their future
together. The answer is simple. They are unwilling to discuss a
solution they did not create and which they do not want. Only
the British government wants it, with perhaps the assent of the
Irish government now in power.

Clearly, if we believe that the problem of Northern Ireland, or
its solution, lies in Northern Ireland only and in some form of
'internal solution', we are being even more naïve now than we
were in the 1960s.

3

A Clerical Society

Ireland is a highly clericalised society in which Christian clergy exert influence both informally and through institutions.

In Northern Ireland Christian clergy are built into the different layers of government. At the top there is the British House of Lords, the highest ranking assembly in the political system. In the House of Lords two archbishops and three bishops have seats by right; twenty-one other bishops are appointed to the House of Lords according to their seniority among the bishops. The number of Christian clergy in the House of Lords may seem to be small, a mere twenty-six among a possible membership of about a thousand. But most of the Lords do not attend regularly and therefore bishops can have considerable influence in the House.

The British Monarch is bound by oath to uphold the rights and privileges of the Protestant Church of England, and since she, with her prime minister, appoints the bishops of the Church of England, there are close and necessary connections between Christian clergymen and the ruling classes and structures in Britain. Further, there are clergy members on the Privy Council. Thus Christian clergy have considerable privilege at the highest levels of government within the British system.

In Northern Ireland itself the two largest political parties, the Official Unionist Party and the Democratic Unionist Party, which are dominated by clergy, command altogether about 54% of votes.

The Official Unionist Party is governed by the Unionist Central Council in which members of the Orange Order have seats by right – the Orange Order is a religious/political organisation in which clergymen are heavily involved; Rev. Martin Smyth who is Grand Master of the Order is a Presbyterian minister who lives in Belfast. The Official Unionist Party is considerably influenced informally also by the Orange Order.

The Democratic Unionist Party was founded by Christian clergymen, and clergy associated with Paisley's Free Presbyterian Church of Ulster are dominant in it.

Of the other parties, none is clerical in this sense. In its early days the Alliance Party (Unionist in politics) was greatly helped by clergymen who believed that some alternative must be found for the existing Unionist parties because they were sectarian and exclusive, but clergy influence in the Alliance Party seems to have no importance now. In 1970 the Social Democratic and Labour Party (SDLP) was founded to take the place of the by then inactive Nationalist Party which had for many years represented the interests of the Catholic community in Northern Ireland. One of the aims of the SDLP was to avoid becoming a clerical party. In the Nationalist Party politicians and Catholic clergy mingled as though they had a common purpose. At conventions for the selection of Nationalist Party candidates the chairman would often be the local parish priest. The SDLP kept its determination not to become a replacement clerical party after the final demise of the Nationalist Party but some efforts have been made by Catholic clergymen to re-establish their influence in the party. For example, at the time of the recent hunger-strikes and the subsequent rise of the Sinn Féin Party, Catholic clergy in a number of places openly, or covertly, supported the SDLP and opposed Sinn Féin.

Management of education is another area in which clergy have a dominating influence. In many Northern Ireland 'state' schools (which deal mainly with Protestant children) the Protestant churches have the right to nominate 'at least 50%' of members to management committees. This means that they have considerable direct influence in policy-making and appointment of teachers at primary and second levels of education. Within the Catholic sector, schools at primary and second level are managed by committees which consist of four nominees of the Catholic churchmen and two nominated by local education authorities. In addition, Catholic clergy controlled until recently the two colleges of education which trained teachers for primary and second level Catholic schools while another, state-run, college of education with a strong, but not dominating, influence of Protestant clergy provided teachers for the state sector.

Further, in the boards set up by the government to manage

education (Education and Library Boards) there are, along with representatives appointed by local authorities, clergymen who are appointed as a matter of policy by the government. Christian clergymen have the right to enter schools in order to teach religious knowledge to children belonging to their religious group.

This presence and influence of Christian clergy in government and education is unique, making Northern Ireland the most clerically influenced area in the European Community. There is considerable political argument about whether the Republic of Ireland or Northern Ireland is the more dominated by clergy. This is an academic exercise because no one has suggested practical ways in which such clerical influence or dominance as there is could be dissolved or modified. Clerical influence is institutionalised in the British Northern Ireland political system and is paralleled by immense informal influence, through press statements, public opinion etc. In the Republic of Ireland Catholic and other clerical influence is built into the institutions of education but not of politics, while informal influence on the public is immense. It would be difficult indeed to decide which of the two areas in Ireland is the more strongly dominated by clergy. But one can say that there is no parallel in any other country in the European Community for the extent and intensity of institutionalised clerical influence in Northern Ireland.

It can be seen, then, that in Ireland the ideology of churchmen must be influential in creating political policies or making or breaking political progress. For example, in the mid-forties there was strong opposition to welfare laws from clergy as well as politicians in Northern Ireland.

In the North of Ireland the issue of separate schools has been kept alive not by parents or teachers but by clergy, as the struggle for separation of schools on religious lines from the 1920s onwards shows. The government of Northern Ireland in the 1920s had a policy of integrating schools and having Catholics, Protestants and others educated together, but opposition from clergy and the Orange Order prevented any such development. If the Protestants had given in, it is only fair to say, Catholic clergy would have taken up the issue and forced the separation of schools in any case.

One can, however, point out that where two kinds of influence exist, namely the institutional and the informal, it is arguably more difficult to dissolve the institutional.

In the Republic of Ireland at present, in the struggle for dominance between clergymen and politicians, the politicians have dissolved to some extent the informally applied influence of clergymen. In the North, however, there seems to be no possibility whatever of anyone being able to dissolve institutional clerical influence applied through the Privy Council, the House of Lords, the area education boards and the clerical political parties. Meanwhile in the North all the mechanisms of informal clerical domination are also effective.

In most issues clergymen are recognised as a powerful force to be reckoned with. It may be a question of liberalising laws about divorce or homosexuality, about Sunday opening of public drinking places; it may be politics, or welfare legislation. On almost every important issue the opinions of the clergy have to be taken into account and are sometimes decisive. While there can be, from time to time, some development in their thinking, and some shifting of ground, this occurs seldom because of the over-riding idealisms which shape the policies of the clergy. Where these idealisms do not change, the political thinking which they inspire does not change either, and thus we find that such unchanging attitudes towards politics, religion and morality beget stagnation and violence. It could be argued that the unchanging quality of life in Northern Ireland owes much to clergymen who as leaders of opinion have placed so much emphasis on constancy and unchangingness as to make these the most desirable virtues. In a distressing situation, however, unchangingness is not necessarily a virtue.

Among Catholic clergy two dominating ideas have shaped their attitudes towards the Republican movement. One of these is fear of Republicanism; the other is fear of Socialism, or any left-wing movement. When a political party or movement unites the two and has a policy of Republican Socialism, or Socialist Republicanism, there is bound to be opposition from the clergy in the Catholic church.

One reason for this seems to be that the experience which the Catholic church had of Socialism in Europe was of a movement which was often anti-clerical, atheist or agnostic. Many bitter antagonisms between clergy and Socialist movements have existed even up to recent times. Socialists need not have been either anti-clerical or atheistic but the historical circumstances in which they found themselves often made them so, while the reaction of the clergy to any attempt to abolish private property, monarchy or the status quo made the Socialist opposition more intense.

Republicanism also was suspect to the European clergy. The Catholic church teaches that it is itself a monarchy, with the Pope as temporal as well as spiritual head of the institution. This idea of the church as a monarchy still exists but is played down nowadays in favour of a more presidential image for the Pope and a more popular appeal by the Church especially to young people. But even as recently as the Second World War there were some clergymen who blamed the ills of the French nation (including defeat by the Germans) on their desertion of the monarchy and the acceptance of a Republic, even though the French revolution was in 1789. In Ireland the historic hero of Republicanism is Wolfe Tone, the Father of Irish Republicanism. Although his memory is revered, Tone was anti-papal, a monarchist and not keen on churches or churchmen. The clergy's perceptions of Socialism and Republicanism, then, are not happy. As recently as the 1930s Catholic clergy in Ireland were asking for help for General Franco's revolution in Spain against, significantly, a government which was left-wing and Republican.

Socialism and Republicanism when translated into Ireland, however, became, broadly speaking, what the Irish wanted them to be. James Connolly, who was a Marxist, found a place for churches, religion and churchmen in his Socialism for a new Ireland. Modern Republicanism, far from being anti-papal, has admitted that religion, churches, and even papacy are founts of idealism too. At the same time they admit that papal policy has been consistently against both Socialism and Republicanism in Ireland.

Political propaganda in Ireland does not always reflect the reality of the situation. For instance, it is said by extreme right-wing Protestants that the Roman Catholic church is the upholder of anti-Britishness, Republicanism and left wing agitation, when the opposite is the case. Republicanism and Socialism have always found their greatest opponents in Ireland among Catholic clergymen, while anti-Britishness was never a noticeable trait of the Irish Catholic clergy in general. At some periods of Irish history a most constant source of information for the British authorities was the clergy scattered over the whole country and enjoying the confidence of the people. When the clergy complained about government they did so against what they considered to be abuses of the system not against the system itself. In general, Catholic church policy in Ireland has been to accept British domination of the country while trying to eliminate abuses and gain concessions for the Church, the clergy or the people. Seldom have high clergy voiced the opinion that the only viable political solution in Ireland is British withdrawal. Recent statements by Cardinal Ó Fiaich are exceptional in modern times. Today it is clear that if an internal solution were available in Northern Ireland, that is, a solution which would keep the area in British control but give a measure of fair government, the Catholic churchmen in general would agree to it. They would probably also condemn armed opposition to such a 'settlement'.

The Protestant churches in Northern Ireland (Anglican, Presbyterian, Methodist principally) are, in general, in favour of the British political system and its hold on Northern Ireland. The united opposition of Protestant churches to radical change has been particularly strong since the mid-nineteenth century. In the eighteenth century Presbyterians experienced hardship from the exactions and oppressions imposed by the Church of Ireland (Anglican) which was at that time the state church in Ireland. Anglican churchmen imposed indignities and oppression upon non-Anglicans, including both Presbyterians and Catholics. When, however, the Presbyterians achieved better treatment they eventually swung over to the side of the Anglicans and the British government. By the end of the nineteenth century the united opposition of practically all Protestant groups against any substantial changes in Ireland was well forged. This opposition showed itself mainly in the form of refusing to accept any kind of independence for Ireland, even of a most limited kind.

Today the Anglican church (Church of Ireland) although it keeps the title of *The* Church of Ireland is no longer a state church, (it was 'disestablished' in 1869). It does, however, publicly support the Unionist cause, against the advice of a small number of its members who live in the Republic of Ireland and a few in the North. The Presbyterians, although they keep some remnants of their former liberal and even Republican ideals, are generally in favour of British rule in Ireland and a policy of keeping down dissent by strong police and military action.

The Methodist church is small and has been traditionally a voice for fairly liberal policies about social welfare etc. Politically, however, Methodists are part of the united opposition of the Protestant churches to any substantial political change in Northern Ireland. The Paisley Church (Free Presbyterian Church of Ulster) was founded as a means of combating the ecumenism of other Protestant groups and to preserve what was seen as the fundamental Protestant political and religious opposition to Romanism, ecumenism, Communism, liberalising laws and political or social change. From this church under the leadership of Rev. Paisley the Democratic Unionist Party was founded.

In the mid-1960s a strong liberalising trend in both the Anglican and Presbyterian churches in Northern Ireland was expressed by a succession of church leaders who tried to create policies of openness toward political and religious opponents. This phase lasted until the mid-1970s when the Presbyterian church reversed the trend and elected severe and uncompromising clergy to leadership while the Anglicans became more and more involved in controversy with Catholics about inter-church marriage, education and politics.

It can be seen from all this that the Christian churches in Northern Ireland are powerful forces, commanding a great deal of respect and resources. They have consistently opposed substantial social and political change and will probably continue to do so in the future. Attendance at church in Northern Ireland, especially in urban areas, is a minority interest (probably between 25% and 40% among Catholics, from 5% to 15% among Protestants). This means that influencing people through the pulpit is less possible than it used to be. Clerical influence exercised through educational institutions, the media, political parties etc. continues and is still very powerful. Public respect accorded to clergymen as men of peace is still very great and the fear of offending the clergy is very real among media people, politicians and others.

If any substantial change is to be made in the political situation in Northern Ireland it would seem, therefore, that the clerical problem will have to be dealt with. But the political parties which are helped by the clergy do not want to destroy this support, while others realise that they would alienate many voters by opposing the clergy. Thus, for example, the Unionist parties and the SDLP rely upon the clergy for moral and often active support, while Sinn Féin, attacked by the clergy of all denominations, are unwilling to lose voters by attacking the clergy too severely in return.

So far, the distinction which has been made in other countries between the institutional Christian church and the popular mass of believers has not made a great impact in Northern Ireland. This distinction is well known of course, and the example of Christian communities elsewhere has been noted and discussed. But the idea of the Christian religion or philosophy being a liberating force is not very strong in Northern Ireland. Christians may at one and the same time look to their churchmen for support in upholding 'law and order' and putting down 'sinful violence', and resent the restrictions which clergy have put upon them and the control they exercise on their lives. So far the possibility that the Christian ideal could be a liberating one has been accepted with, at best, reservation and at worst outright scepticism. For many Christians forgiveness and love are not seen as a means of bringing about peace. On the contrary, they say that forgiveness and love can only be exercised when a firm framework of law and order has been established by the state's military and police. Within that framework of law and order Christians can then fulfil their duty to love each other. Without the framework of law and order imposed by force the Christians are powerless and are reduced to simply supporting the state and its military actions until such time as they succeed in defeating the enemies of the state.

To other Christians this idea of the meaning and function of Christian forgiveness and love is bizarre and unacceptable; for the majority of Christians in Northern Ireland, however, it is a normal attitude which helps decide Christian policies towards the state, military, police and dissident political groups. Clearly the fresh thinking of liberation theology groups has little place in a situation of this kind. It is remotely possible that the idealism of Christian liberation theology could, if properly understood and discussed in Northern Ireland, help to break the mould but, unfortunately, the low intellectual level of political and religious discussion makes such a possibility very remote indeed.

For anyone living in such a situation as that of Northern Ireland the work of bringing about social, political or religious change is daunting. One cannot affect the institutions directly. One can experiment, hoping that each experiment, however small, will show that there is an alternative way of life, alternative politics, and alternative religious or philosophical ideals. There have been a number of such experiments in Northern Ireland.

At different times during the past sixteen years groups of citizens have created alternative and more independent forms of education, Lagan College (an independent integrated school), An Scoil Ghaelach (an independent Irish speaking school), the Open College (for adults seeking open and liberal education courses), the Ulster People's College (trade union based, for an open and free education in which people may see the real reasons for their economic and social situation and thus be able to do something creative about it), free schools for children etc. Some of these experiments have not survived, such as the Open College, but enough of them have survived to make the idea of an alternative to the existing state/religious education system seem viable.

There have also been attempts to create alternative media: Paisley's newspaper was set up in opposition to existing Unionist newspapers, there is an Irish language daily paper, *Lá*, the first ever daily newspaper in the Irish language; free radio stations were quickly set up in the upheavals of 1969–70 but were suppressed; a recent attempt to set up an Irish language radio station based in Belfast failed for technical reasons. Alternative policing and alternative military forces have both been tried and in the case of the second of these the experiment is still going on as the military conflict between armed Republicans and British military forces shows. Indeed one can understand much of what happens in Northern Ireland as attempts by people to set up alternatives to existing institutions which have proved to be unjust and unacceptable. Some of the experiments succeed and many fail. Attempts to create jobs through co-operatives have been a constant feature of life in Ireland for many years and people who have been engaged in them often explain that their success or failure as business ventures is not the whole story. Succeeding or failing commercially, they always succeeded educationally because participants learned about business, about money and about the resources which they had scant knowledge of and which the government carefully concealed from them.

By means of all these experiments in a very tense and often volatile political situation people in Northern Ireland, especially in the poorer areas, became politically aware and politically active to a degree which neither political nor religious leaders seemed able to comprehend. The rise of Sinn Féin was another example of people, especially in these poor areas, creating an alternative, this time a political party. Northern Ireland provides a fascinating case study of people who in a short space of time and often with great intensity involved themselves in the business of creating an impressive variety of alternatives.

A serious question which faces Christians in this situation in Ireland is whether they wish to contribute anything to creating alternative politics, alternative economics, alternative military and police, alternative education and worship. At first glance it seems that one can only be pessimistic, because both in theory and in practice Christians are highly conservative. Experience shows that even when faced with a shameful and degrading situation the Christian clergy still keep their devotion to the status quo. Indeed the status quo has been invested by the Christians with a kind of divine sanction as if changing it would bring further evils from an angry god. Yet it is in many cases individual Christians who have been engaged in the day-to-day work of creating all these alternatives. It is very mistaken to believe that experiments in creating a new military force have been made only by men and women who have forsaken their Christian ways for the ways of sin, as many clergymen would have us believe. Some of the people who took up arms for either Republican or Loyalist causes in Northern Ireland were among the most dedicated and loyal of Christians with deep feelings of loyalty to their Christian communities. What the British government describes as terrorism by thugs and criminals is in reality the desperate response of good people who believe that there are limits to the insults which they can be expected to endure. One should not under-estimate the moral quality of people who take up arms and it is well to reflect that broadly speaking the only body of people in Northern Ireland who have taken up arms for money are the British forces. Many of those who took up arms for the Loyalist or Republican cause have given up a great deal as a result, freedom, health, family life or life itself. Needless to say, the burden has fallen mostly on the Republican side. One of the problems facing the clergymen is,

* Key point/observation

then, to distinguish between those who seem to take up a cause but in reality are simply helping themselves, and those who take up a cause because they believe in it so much that they are prepared to suffer for it. One of the tragedies of the Christian churches in Ireland is that they have not been able to make that distinction. In their anxiety to be on the right side they have often discarded what should have been their greatest power, namely the discerning of spirits, the ability to distinguish between good and evil.

Some religious groups have seen the situation for what it is, the lining up of immense forces, which are all essentially Christian, in a struggle for power which has distorted Christian values and flung the Christians in Ireland into a state of crisis.

One of the difficulties the Christians have, however, is that so far they have had immense difficulty in identifying what exactly the crisis is and, therefore, what they should do about it.

The immense resources of the Christians, their great political and cultural experience, their wealth, their international relationships, are today being used in Northern Ireland as they have been used in the past, not to make peace by bringing about a new political creation but to preserve the past with its distortion of values and its violence.

It may not be a religious struggle in Northern Ireland but it is a struggle all the more violent and intractable because of its religious dimensions.

↳ Another good point.

4

Violence – Theirs and Ours

ONE OF the constant problems in Northern Ireland is that of the police. They were never merely protectors of person and property, they were protectors of the state and of the political party which ran it.

To say, as many of us do, that the problem of the police is one of thirty or forty unscrupulous members is to avoid the problem. Unscrupulous members do exist but given proper control they are not a great problem. Bad policemen under strict and honourable control can be reasonably good watchdogs – but good policemen under unscrupulous political control will become as bad as their masters. That is to say, policing is not a problem of Northern Ireland, it is a universal problem in every place where police are under centralised political control. It is the political control of the police that is the problem.

It is natural for people who have suffered false imprisonment, torture or other forms of abuse to believe that evil individual officers are the root of the problem, but it is a misunderstanding. If enough people believe it, though, then a government can pretend that its own process of 'weeding out the evil-doers' will solve the problem of the police oppression, when they know very well that it will not. A party in power will be tempted to use as many of the resources of the state as it can in order to stay in power. The police are one resource and in some political situations, including those in Ireland, it would take superhuman virtue not to use them as such, especially in what is in effect a one party state, as Northern Ireland was from 1922 until 1972. Police can slip easily and even unwittingly from their role as guardians of person and property into that of guardians of a political party which is in power and wants to stay there. It happened so smoothly in the North that one is justified in suggesting that it could happen just as smoothly in the rest of Ireland too if citizens do not prevent it.

In Ireland we think this is a foreign problem because we have seen it so often elsewhere. Because it happens so often in other places we should have recognised it as a universal problem of political life. It cannot be democratic to allow one set of vested interests to control the police – for example, the merchants or the churchmen. It cannot be democratic to allow one political party to do it, as was the case in Northern Ireland in the past and as Unionist leaders demand it should be the case in the future. Nor can we allow that as soon as a political party comes to power it thereby necessarily gains access to the police as a means of supporting itself and curbing its enemies, a situation which seems to have arisen in Britain and the Republic of Ireland. You may use the police to beat the miners in Britain or to beat Republicans in Ireland but the purpose in both cases is similar, to destroy what is seen as a threat not to public morality but to political parties.

One of the few safeguards against this could be control of the police by specially elected bodies of people in local areas who, after all, pay the police to protect them. There have been discussions about setting up police authorities but these have not been about giving local people power to curb or control police, although they seem to be so. The experiment of a Police Authority in the North with members from a wide range of citizens on it has not been a success. The Police Authority was in effect a support for the government's use of police rather than a critic of the police. The government and police dominated the Authority, not the other way round. Citizens who found themselves without adequate statutory safeguards against abuses were then reduced – since the Police Authority existed and did not work – to asking the government to set up inquiries. The usefulness of the inquiry procedure from the government point of view is that while people are discussing whether there should be an inquiry or not into particular incidents, and even as a result of such an inquiry itself, public indignation cools. The government's position is made safe but abuses are neither rectified nor prevented. A Police Authority of the kind set up in Northern Ireland is not a protection for citizens, it is an instrument of government.

In the North of Ireland there have been many calls for changes of personnel in the police, for inquiries into the police and for changes in the procedures of police work. There has been no significant demand for changes in political party or central government control, or for control by local people among whom the police work or by whom they are paid. Local police authorities with real powers are not being demanded by anyone. Yet it can be doubted if reform of police' forces is possible without some such radical changes. And that problem is not a peculiarly Irish one.

The system of emergency laws is not a specially Irish one, either. There is a well-tried procedure which governments use when they want to introduce an oppressive law. The public is made aware of a serious crisis, real or not. The need for emergency laws – temporary laws – to meet the crisis is stressed by politicians and other opinion leaders, churchmen, the media etc., and is, therefore, accepted by people in general. The laws are passed quickly. (They may have been in preparation for some time, awaiting a suitable opportunity to be introduced.) When the crisis is over, or said to be over, the emergency laws remain and will be used in the future to deal with 'ordinary' crime or with groups who are offensive to the government. The Offences Against the State Act is an Irish example.

Some emergency laws were introduced in the Dáil in a wave of hysteria following bombings which were seen to be the work not of Irish 'subversives' but of British agents. In the North of Ireland emergency laws were always a permanent feature of the legal system – belief in the need for them was sustained for many years by reiterated propaganda about the ever-present IRA. Most of the period from the 1920s until the Second World War, however, saw the IRA in the North in a very weak position, with neither the organisation nor the arms – nor the public support – to sustain a rebellion. Each generation of Republicans, though, had to make a gesture, even if it only meant firing off the few shotguns they had at various points in any one county. The small capacity of citizens to rebel was out of all proportion to the massive penalties for doing it. Police forces created for the preservation of the state were kept at work for the preservation of a political party. The striking thing about emergency laws and emergency police anywhere is their sameness, permanency, and severity. The last man to be flogged by judicial sentence in the North of Ireland for Republicanism is still alive in Belfast.

The development of police and crisis laws in post-war West

Germany is an example away from home. Border guards who, the public was told, were specially tough and confined to guard duty at the border between east and west were gradually drawn away from the border and inserted into normal structures of policing. Their toughness remained and so did the laws which brought them into existence. The Prevention of Terrorism Act in Britain, because it was directed against the Irish, was not seen for what it is, a licence for extremely severe and arbitrary procedures which one day can be used against anyone in Britain as the government of the day decides.

The tendency of people in Ireland to discuss policing or emergency laws as if they were the product of some Irish quirk or disease has made it difficult to raise the discussion to a useful level. Discussing the moral character of a garda or constable does not solve what are international, not just local, human organisational problems. Any useful discussion about law and policing should not only be about what the citizens or even the police are up to – it should also be about what the government is up to, which may be a much more important question.

Emergency laws can be used to deal with offences for which emergency laws are not necessary. People can be arrested and charged – and held – under laws which were, it was said, created to deal only with political subversion, even though there is no question of political action involved. How easily the public accepts this is seen by their failure to react to it – there seems to them nothing strange in hearing an RTE commentator, for example, described as a 'security correspondent' when what he is describing is house robberies in County Mayo. Protection of the state against external enemies, protection against internal enemies and action against crime are made to appear as if they were the same thing. In this process an ambitious government's best ally is an indifferent citizen. In the North of Ireland a citizen can be arrested and held in custody because military or police want this to be done for their own reasons. Real suspicion of having committed a crime need not be present.

When I brought a case against the British army in 1980 I lost. The judge told the court that British soldiers could arrest anyone, as they arrested me, without any question of a crime being committed. Certainly, he said, there had to be in the mind of the arresting soldier a real suspicion, but this suspicion could be put

there by a superior officer who need just say to him, 'Arrest that
man, I suspect him.' Of course, the officer need not have a real
suspicion at all, but in order to make such an arrest legal it was
sufficient to plant a suspicion in the arresting soldier's mind;
needless to say a soldier is not going to question a superior officer
about whether his suspicion is real or not. It was an extraordinary
judgement and one which illustrates the nature of British police
and military powers against which the courts were useless because
the legislators had made bad law. People can be accused, and have
been, under the 'supergrass' system, of charges such as 'having
conspired at dates unknown with persons unknown to murder a
person or persons unknown.' As has been pointed out by lawyers,
it is impossible to defend oneself against a charge like this. If we
were to read about such a thing in a book by Kafka we would
shudder and say, 'Thank God it is not real.' It is real in Northern
Ireland and will continue to be real until the legislators who create
such possibilities are no longer in power. Those who are held
without access to spiritual or material comforting, without legal
advice and uncertain about what they are to be charged with or
what is to become of them could perhaps bear this with patience
if they thought it was for the good of the whole people; but that
it should be done for the safety of a regime or a political party
which is running a state in which injustice is irredeemable adds
bitterness indeed. The degeneration of legal systems into
procedures of this kind can be swift and calamitous. In the North
of Ireland it was so. It is ironical that what was imposed by force
on the people of the North is being accepted by the people of the
South of Ireland of their own free will. The Republic's legal
procedures are swiftly descending to the British level.

It could be argued that the creation of repressive laws will in
the long run do more damage to citizens than the political activity
they were meant to prevent.

The kind of laws passed in any state depend not only on the
benefit the citizens should enjoy in the future but also on who
holds real power in the situation now, and in whose interest they
hold it. We do not know just how much power resides in the
British House of Commons, how much lies in the British cabinet
where a prime minister can dictate to a compliant table of
ministers or can impose policies through strict party discipline.
More seriously, how much power resides in British institutions

outside parliament altogether, how much in the civil service, military or business establishments. It is a question sometimes mentioned in Britain but seldom discussed possibly because it would be unpleasant and worrying to find out. In Britain the absence of a written constitution is a difficulty; there is no clear statement about power on which one can base a judgement or a case. It is interesting to note that the most pointed questions being raised about the British system and the influence of the civil service, the BBC etc. are being raised in a television programme entitled *Yes Minister* and not in newspapers or in parliament. It is in a way a modern British version of the Irish custom of solving an intractable problem by laughing at it, because you are powerless to deal with it otherwise.

It is proper to ask, too, whether events in Ireland are a response to the needs of some British establishment rather than to those of the whole people of Ireland. We do not often ask such a question. This is not because we are not aware that such questions should be asked, for after all we are constantly asking whether what politicians do about divorce, contraception etc. is dictated by the needs of an external ecclesiastical power or by our own needs. If we can ask such questions in one context we can ask them in another. To be master of our own house we need to be master not only of the prayer room but of the kitchen and the room where the safe is kept. If what we are doing is dictated by the neighbour's needs and not ours we are right to feel resentful and to make changes. Rushing emergency laws through the Dáil to the sound of other people's bombs should have made us question the motivation or wisdom of the legislators. Strangely enough, we talk easily about satellite nations so much under the sway of the Soviets that they can make no decisions of their own, while the idea that satellites may exist in the western capitalist world and that we may be one of them is never discussed at all. Whose power moves us economically, religiously, politically or in any other way?

There need be no reasonable doubt that the British government wishes to remain in control of some part of Ireland; or at least that powerful interested parties in Britain wish to do so. That being so, it is unlikely that a solution to the problem of Northern Ireland can be obtained simply through reasoning with British politicians. Irish politicians who wish to change our present relationship with the British government must discover where the real power lies there, and what importance is to be attached to each element in the British political system, to the monarchy, aristocracy, state church, army, cabinet, House of Commons, business interests, etc.

Military Republicans have decided that the real power of the British connection in Ireland is a military one and that if this can be neutralised then the other elements can be forced to negotiate. It is in this context that the Republican military campaign can be seen. It would be, they say, useless to confront the British cabinet or the British House of Commons without at the same time confronting the British army, which could well frustrate them both and, in any case, it is the repressive force which makes it possible for the government to maintain its hold on the area.

To dismiss what military Republicans are doing simply as 'terrorism' is to hide the true nature of what is happening. To dismiss it simply as 'mindless' is to refuse to analyse it adequately and therefore to risk being mindless ourselves.

Those who are struggling against an unjust political system must try all honourable and peaceful means to bring about change. When, however, all of these have proved ineffective what can they do? They can either invent new non-military means of making political progress or go to war. In the Irish situation every available peaceful means of change has failed: Nationalist participation in a predominantly Unionist parliament, appeals to reason, to Westminster, appeals over the heads of politicians by demonstrations in the streets, appeals to churchmen and to international opinion. 'Initiatives' created by successive British governments in Northern Ireland since 1969 have also failed.

At present, British and Irish politicians say that no radical initiatives are now possible because they would not succeed, and the best that can be done is to create very limited consultative arrangements which will recognise the dignity of the parties concerned in the dispute, but will make no substantial political or economic changes. It is an admission that we are in an intractable situation for which governments and, therefore much more, citizens have by common admission no solution. Unless we can create fresh and useful non-military means of producing effective change it is illogical to condemn those who resort to arms against a government which cannot or will not solve the problems of injustice and yet insists upon keeping intact the structures of government which caused the injustices in the first place. The armed citizens who fight the government in Northern Ireland could well say that there are no effective peaceful initiatives left; and the two governments involved would have to agree with them. There is a rational argument, not one from emotion, for refusing to condemn those who take up arms in such a situation. If the situation changes and it appears that non-military means are available and would be effective in creating justice in Northern Ireland then one would have to revise this view. In the meantime, condemnation is appropriate only if it can be shown that real possibilities of creating justice exist and can be put into operation.

There need not be any inconsistency in refusing to condemn citizens who use arms in such a situation while at the same time condemning a government for using arms against the citizens. The citizens may have no alternative ways of pressing for justice; a government always has alternative ways of governing in order to create justice. We want to stop the war; victory over military Republicans is impossible and would be in any case a postponement not a settlement; if we want to condemn those who use arms we shall have to be able to show that non-military means are available to dissolve the injustices of British activity in Ireland; if such means do not exist we have to admit it and, if we can, begin to invent new non-military means which will be effective.

What is in question in Ireland is the creation of a modern democracy or the refusal to create one. The war could, in theory, be ended by either the defeat of the Republican military movement or the creation of a powerful non-military political movement so strong that military means would be seen to be unnecessary.

Like many others in the North of Ireland now I have fewer inhibitions about making my own view of the matter clearer than I would have had ten or twenty years ago. I believe that it is the moral duty of citizens to remove the root cause of injustices in the North of Ireland, the British government, and to replace it by a modern democratic government of the Irish people's own choosing – a reform of the British system which would make it into an acceptable modern democracy is not likely and in any case it would take too long.

At the same time I cannot reconcile being a priest with being a member of any particular political party. A priest must be open

to all who want to have anything to do with him – membership
of a party involves an exclusiveness which is unacceptable. But
believing that I and other citizens have a moral duty to help create
a modern democracy in Ireland I also believe that churchmen in
general have a similar duty, and Catholic churchmen in particular,
since it is the Catholic people who have been most disadvantaged
by the British regime imposed on them. Involving churches or
churchmen in politics is a delicate business – you have to make
them interfere, but at the same time curb them so that they can
never interfere too much, insisting upon their interference now
and upon their non-interference later in the democracy which they
will help to create. What is happening in the South of Ireland,
the continuing contest between churchmen and politicians far
from being a bad thing makes us hope that the healthy curbing
process is already under way there, and that politicians and
churchmen will as time goes on act as a restraining influence on
each other. In the North the Catholic churchmen have scarcely
begun to oppose the regime.

The British government, however, is already showing signs of
changing its policy of giving certain financial support to the
hierarchy as part of a 'gentleman's agreement' that the hierarchy
will act as a controlling influence on the people. Catholic churchmen were told they must close one of their colleges of education
and the government has severely reduced the scope of work done
in what was left.

Churchmen must recognise that governments support them not
because they want to but because they have to, for the sake of the
stability of the state. This support may disappear as the government begins to recognise that churches are not as potent control-
lers of people's political lives as they used to be. Churchmen have
to recognise also that state support may be bought at too high a
price and that there is little use in controlling an education system
in what can never become a modern democracy with acceptable
standards of justice. They will only have connived at evil.

Governments understand political violence only in the sense of
taking up arms against them. They do not acknowledge that much
of what is done to citizens is violence too. Churchmen in Ireland
generally accept the vocabulary of government without question.
They say, for example, that 'since 1969 we have had violence in
Northern Ireland' – that is a moral and political judgement that

what went before 1969 – the gerrymandering, the flogging, the exile, the death – were not violent. Such a use of language is not a tool of analysis as we like to pretend; it is a weapon to oppress by pretending that violence is what the citizen does, force is what the government uses and one is bad, the other good.

About sixty countries have been identified as using torture for information gathering; Britain which rules part of Ireland is one of them. If torture of this kind and other abuses are included in the term 'violence' then the only answer we could make to those who ask us to outlaw violence would be, 'By all means let us outlaw violence, everybody's violence.' It is worse than useless, however, to outlaw one man's violence if in so doing you help another's to flourish.

Selective condemnation of violence in the restricted sense of armed action against governments can have a tragic result. It can help to strengthen the oppressive hand of governments who may have little other sanction against them than the armed revolt of their citizens, all peaceful means having failed. By condemning one kind of violence we may unwittingly help to perpetuate another. Churchmen in Ireland have often forced themselves into that postion. Having accepted the government's definitions of what words like 'violence' mean they can only use those words as the governments want them to, not necessarily as Christ might want them to. They could do more for morality by keeping a dignified silence or at least by defining their terms before they speak.

To those whose only desire is to stop the war in Ireland one can say, 'If you destroy the Republican military movement today the British government will still be there to do what it has always done, impose bad government by force; remove the British government and the Republican military movement will cease to exist.' Disbandment of the Republican military movement does not solve the problem; removal of the British government makes a solution possible.

Against this some people argue that if the British government leaves Ireland there will be a bloodbath. Others maintain that if the military Republicans are not defeated they will impose a Marxist Republic on Ireland. As to the first of these, it is worthwhile to think about the words of a Loyalist paramilitary leader who when asked about such a possibility said, 'And who do you think would fight a war if a war had to be fought? We would. And do you think we would fight a war to put Paisley and Smyth in power? We won't.' They probably won't either. Unionists have never during the past hundred years fought unless they had the forces of the State on their side. It is unlikely they will now. Their policy has always been not to fight against the forces of the State but to ensure that the forces of the State were on their side. The 1912-14 Loyalist adventure does not contradict this because the Loyalist leaders knew that they would not be opposed by British military or police. The mobilisation, covenant, the gun-running, the whole campaign of the signing of the covenant was as much an awareness-raising campaign as a serious attempt to create a military movement. Recent statements by politicians like Mr Molyneaux show this same tendency – he refused to commit people to the paramilitaries, but a large part of the political life of people like him has been devoted to keeping the forces on their side. It is not impossible that in the event of a British decision to remove themselves from Ireland Loyalists with the help of the UDR and RUC would withdraw into territory which they can hold in the east of Ulster and would use their holding of this territory as a bargaining counter, not as a place where they would permanently settle as in a kind of reservation. They have never fought in Ireland without the state's armed forces in front of them and there is no good reason to believe that the pattern will change. Significantly, the final end of the forces mustered to oppose Home Rule was that they were shepherded into the British regular army and sent off to the Somme. They had done all they were required to do at home.

As to the argument that a Marxist state will be set up by force if the British government leaves, it is worth remarking that all the oppressions of which Irish people have first hand knowledge were imposed by Christians not by Marxists. And that adherence of Irish political activists to Marxism is so tenuous that Irish people will in all probability for many years to come do as they have always done – use what freedom they have to elect extremely conservative political assemblies. The Dáil and the Northern Ireland Assembly are examples of what Irish people do with a free vote. A radical in either of them must feel as lonely as St Paul in a roomful of feminists.

Another, more plausible, objection to the removal of British

rule from Ireland is that Protestants would lose the protection and
status which the British regime gives them. It is an objection
which has to be taken seriously, and part of any settlement must
be honourable protection of all minorities. Practising Catholics
could well become a minority in Ireland too and in some places
are well on the way to becoming that already. But at least in a
future settlement there is hope for a new dignity for Protestants;
the British regime did not protect them effectively, although it
claimed to exist for that purpose. The British regime existed to
protect financial and strategic interests. The regime showed a cyn-
ical disregard for the interests of Protestant citizens in that it
placed them in the necessary role of defenders of the indefensible,
defenders on the spot of goods enjoyed by others at a distance.
What was protected on the Shankill Road was enjoyed in London,
a classic imperialist situation. To this day London enjoys a good
reputation among Irish people and the Shankill a bad one. It
should be the other way around.

Catholic Republicans find it hard to convince their Protestant
fellow citizens, though, that they are really fighting for Protestant
freedom as well as their own and that the proper thing would be
for both to fight for freedom together. If they did, then an armed
campaign might well still take place because the British government is concerned to prevent subversion of its position in Ireland,
no matter who the subversives might be. Even as it is there are
many Protestants in gaol.

Protestant Republicans, and there are some, want freedom but
do not want to be swamped in a Catholic state. It would not be a
pleasant situation, given that the Irish Catholic state would have
ideas of democracy roughly the same as those of the British.

In this kind of situation where one is dissatisfied with what
one has but always afraid of what one may get in its place,
reasonable argument, based on sound analysis and therefore on
good definitions is urgently needed. The British government does
not clarify matters for its own supporters or for democrats.
It blurs and obscures them. Like any government which holds
on too long, it is eventually met with the same kind of force as it
uses itself and pretends that evil characters rather than bad
government are responsible. The surprising thing is not that a
counter military action recently took on such force in the North
of Ireland; rather that it did not come sooner and with even

greater force.

And that more Protestants were not part of it.

5

Sinn Féin and Its Vote

The re-entry of Sinn Féin into Northern Ireland politics as a serious contender for the votes of the anti-Unionists from 1982 onwards was dramatic and revelatory. Dramatic because it meant the rejection by a large number of people of clear directions given to them by the church and state that they should not vote for the party; revelatory because as Sinn Féin consolidated its position one could see what other parties and institutions understood by democracy.

The analysis made by Mr Nkrumah (*Handbook of Revolutionary Warfare*, 1968) of the colonial and post-colonial situation in emerging African countries would be recognised by Irish people: a colonial power favours one native political party not because it wishes to strengthen it but in order to weaken another party which it looks upon as a greater threat. In Northern Ireland after the significant electoral performance of Sinn Féin the Social Democratic and Labour Party was more acceptable than heretofore. It was at times even praised by members of the British regime, favours were promised (but never given) and the moderation of the SDLP was contrasted starkly against the extremism of Sinn Féin. Some favours had already come from Dublin to strengthen the SDLP, limited membership of Seanad Éireann, membership of the Forum for a New Ireland (1983). Meanwhile Sinn Féin was more and more abused, harassed and condemned by both British and Irish governments.

One could look at this as governmental encouragement of moderation in politics had there been any concrete concessions to the SDLP to prove it. But there were none, and even membership of Seanad Éireann was seen to be carefully controlled as the FitzGerald government replaced Senator Mallon by Mrs Brid Rogers when it had a chance to do so (1983). One could also see it as Mr Nkrumah saw similar governmental favours and

rejections in emerging African states. The SDLP was tolerable,
Sinn Féin was not. Sinn Féin was the greatest danger to the
colonial power. But neither party was likely to be given what it
wanted.

When, against advice from politicians and churchmen, voters
insisted on drawing Sinn Féin into the political arena in successive
elections in Northern Ireland politicians of other parties
trivialised the vote it had won. It was, they said, a frustration
vote, a vote against bad housing and unemployment, it was a vote
got by personation. But people who are simply frustrated do not
vote at all. It was recognised that probably many of Sinn Féin's
voters had not voted before because they felt they had nothing to
vote for; it was a strange frustration that drove people to the polls
rather than away from them.

The simplest and probably most accurate explanation of the
large vote given to Sinn Féin in recent Northern Ireland elections
is that this was a mandate from voters to solve the British problem
if possible by non-military means, if necessary by military means.
The Sinn Féin Party had gone to the polls unequivocally supporting an armed campaign against the British government and its
voters could not have been in doubt as to what their vote meant.

For many people it was a stark and frightening vote, and
churchmen in particular recognised the meaning of it. Catholic
churchmen had urged voters not to vote for Sinn Féin and many
Catholics disobeyed them. It was not a matter only of
disobedience; it was a matter of moral theology.

The Catholic church has strict rules about when a revolution
is justified and when it is not. For example, say the moralists, a
revolution must have a reasonable chance of success. But the post-
factum acceptance of the 1916 Revolution showed that for
Catholic churchmen success did not mean necessarily immediate
success. In the North of Ireland by 1979 even British army
officers admitted that they were facing a sophisticated enemy who
if defeated now would certainly begin again in the future. The
best they could foresee for themselves was a lull not a victory.
Another condition is that a revolution has to be mandated by the
people. Politicians and churchmen argued that the military
Republicans had no mandate at all. Now it appeared that as many
as 40% or more of Nationalist voters were prepared to vote for
Sinn Féin. If the vote became any larger – even if it stayed much

the same – could it not be said that the revolution of the Republicans was approved by many of the people? At least it now seemed to be approved by a large proportion of those who suffered most under the regime, and the case for outright condemnation on the basis of Catholic theology was not as strong as it seemed. Propaganda could no longer say that they had no mandate at all; it was possible that one day theologians would have to admit that they had a mandate after all. Before that day comes, the British and Irish politicians and churchmen believe that Sinn Féin has to be destroyed by any means available. They must be prevented from getting a mandate, otherwise the last condition laid down by the Catholic moralists would be seen to have been fulfilled.

It was understandable that the Catholic churchmen should try to prevent people voting for Sinn Féin and once they had done it to trivialise the vote so that it did not seem like a mandate for the military struggle at all. The implications of the vote – and the popular mandate – were frightening and theologically troubling.

But churchmen have to be true to their own theology. There were some clergy who by 1975 were admitting privately that nearly all the conditions required by Catholic theology for a justified revolution were present in Northern Ireland. A reasonable chance of success and a mandate were lacking, yet they continued to condemn the Republican military campaign on the grounds that although the two missing conditions were rapidly being fulfilled also their task as parish clergy was to pass on to the people a message for which local bishops, not they, were responsible. The emergence of the large Sinn Féin vote showed that there was a significant difference of opinion among Catholics in general, a difference of opinion which already existed among clergy but had been hidden by the doctrine of the supremacy of obedience to episcopal authority. At some time that theological bubble may burst.

The difficulty for churchmen was that refusing to condemn the Republicans' armed campaign seemed to commit them to approving of war, and this they were unwilling to do. But it did not necessarily commit them to war. It would have committed them to the task of helping to create a non-military political movement to bring about radical change in the North of Ireland. Catholic churchmen were in the unhappy position of uttering condemnations which their theology did not quite justify while being afraid to commit themselves to what their theology *did* justify, namely the demand for justice expressed in a fresh political movement.

For many churchmen, helping to create a fresh political movement would have meant aligning themselves with the aims of Sinn Féin and even with its policies, and this was unthinkable. The government said that those who agreed with Sinn Féin's view must be supporters of the IRA and therefore immoral. Catholic churchmen accepted this view instead of taking a view of their own which would have been in better accord with their theology. The logic of the government's argument was as faulty as if one said: Paisley believes in God, and is anti-Catholic, therefore anyone who believes in God is helping Paisley and must be anti-Catholic; we must, therefore, stop believing in God. The churchmen have never accepted, however, that they might have a moral duty to create a fresh political movement of opposition to the British government as the only practical way of ending the war.

For pacifists in this situation there seemed to be no arguments left by 1980. If all honourable means had been used and if those who should have been intent on ending the war were unwilling to create the political pressure necessary to make that happen, what could the pacifists say? It seemed hypocritical to call oneself a pacifist and yet not condemn those who used arms, but, paradoxically, to refuse to condemn the use of arms by citizens until the government created justice could be a valid contribution to peace. Will Warren, a member of the Society of Friends, spent many years in Derry where he came to the conclusion that just condemning people was worse than useless; his discussions with various parties in the dispute, rather than his condemnation of them, would, he said, have made his Quaker friends bring him back home to England if they misunderstood them as badly as did some of the people in the North of Ireland.

It would seem that the British government is content that the war in Ireland should continue, provided that the destructiveness of it can be contained. Most of the Christian clergy who have spoken about the matter want the defeat of the Republican movement. Pacifists want an end to the war, but there are few pacifists. It is not surprising then that the destruction of the Republican movement has become more important to many people than the ending of the war – and the two things are not the same. Unionists in recent elections could not think of a more convincing electoral slogan than, 'Smash Sinn Féin'. The negative ideal is the only one that counts because it is the only one understood.

When Sinn Féin became a serious contender for the votes of Nationalist people in Northern Ireland the greatest argument used against the party was that it advocated 'violence'. What it advocated was a military struggle against the British government in so far as such a struggle was needed. Clergymen opposed Sinn Féin with vigour and in so doing Catholic churchmen placed themselves in a position in which they could not win: if Sinn Féin lost then the churchmen would be blamed, if they won, then the churchmen would be seen to be ineffective. They had made a moral issue of it and when more than 40% of Catholic voters voted for Sinn Féin it was clear that the Catholic church was split on what had been described as a serious moral issue. According to traditional Catholic moral theology, when there is a serious difference of opinion about the interpretation of a moral principle, the people cannot be bound to the more strict interpretation. That is, by a principle of Catholic theology it would no longer be possible to unreservedly condemn the vote for Sinn Féin. Certainly the traditional church view was that a difference of opinion between *experts* was what was in question, but the truth was that many churchmen saw nothing immoral in voting for Sinn Féin because in voting every person has to make up his or her own mind. In effect, Catholics were making up their own moral principles, or making their own interpretation of moral principles, whatever the churchmen might say. Had the course of events since the rise of Sinn Féin been discussed openly and in the light of traditional Catholic beliefs the discussion would have revealed the presence of a theological crisis within the Catholic church. The crisis existed but was never faced; churchmen gradually had to come to terms with the fact that in this matter their writ did not run and open general condemnation of Sinn Féin on the Catholic side practically ceased in the run up to local council elections in May 1984, although there were still some areas where clerical opposition remained confidently public.

The general opposition to Sinn Féin also revealed what other people meant by democracy. For the Northern Ireland Unionist it meant the careful construction of a majority and having majority rule from there on. But for modern democrats democracy means more than this, it means not only majority rule but a share for each citizen in government. This second element in a modern democracy has never been conceded by Unionists: if the constructed majority should dissolve for any reason then a fresh majority may have to be constructed and the process begun again. The carving out of the six north-eastern counties of Ireland created the first majority for Unionists; by 1985 the creation of a fresh majority was being discussed, that is re-partition and continuing British occupation of an area east of the River Bann, approximately two counties in place of six, in which for some years to come there would be a secure Unionist majority in a small population. This kind of solution was being discussed among Unionists while the British government was on the one hand trying to destroy Sinn Féin and on the other trying to build up a reasonably contented but powerless Catholic lower middle class.

Such a second partition would be equally undemocratic not only because it would go against the wishes of the Irish people as a whole but also because it would still deny the second of the two elements of democracy, a part for all citizens in the government of their own country.

Normally the ability of voters to change the party in power is a safeguard against citizens being permanently excluded from government; those excluded in one election can hope for a better result next time. In Britain some of those who consistently voted for the Liberal Party understood the frustration of people in Northern Ireland who were perpetually excluded from government. So were, in effect, the Liberals in Britain. But the Liberals in Britain had a remedy which could work within their political system; they formed the Liberal/SDP Alliance with the result that participation in government became a possibility. In Northern Ireland, however, there was an exclusion from government which was permanent and unchangeable because it was impossible constitutionally to pass the government over from one party to another. The right of every citizen to have a share in government has never been conceded by the Unionists in Northern Ireland; attempts by successive British governments to persuade them to concede it have failed.

The situation has its own ironies. All during the period of the

Stormont regime (1921–1972) about 40% of the population – the Catholic part – had been told that they would have none of the rights and privileges of political life. This was the response of Unionist administrations to the Nationalist and other non-Unionist parties. The response of the Irish political parties and of Irish churchmen in the South to those who voted for Sinn Féin was that they would have none of the rights or privileges of political life either – elected representatives would be left standing outside the gates of Leinster House, would not be allowed to meet ministers of state, would receive none of the courtesies of political life – and about 40% of Catholic voters in the North had voted for the Sinn Féin party there. It was a curious coincidence, this 40%, and one which made it clear that the standard of democracy to be expected from Irish political parties and churchmen was much the same as they already received from the British.

Catholics in the North were faced once again with the all too familiar spectre of disenfranchisement, this time also by those whom they had believed were in some sense their own people. Many became alienated not only from the British administration but from Irish politicians and churchmen as well. For the first time in many years some Catholics were thinking in the way Loyalists had been thinking in the early 1970s – discovering they could no longer trust the British and unwilling to trust fellow Irish people either.

In Ireland as in Britain there was one other principle of democracy which had never been accepted, namely the absolute right of people to be heard through elected representatives of their own choice. That this was so came as a surprise to many people, and if the rise of Sinn Féin did nothing else it demonstrated how primitive both Irish and British ideas of democracy actually are. The democratic principle is clear and we are presumed to accept it: one may approve or not of a political party, one may try to persuade the party to change or the people not to vote for it, but once the choice is made at the polls the people's right to be heard through those whom they have freely elected is absolute. It does not depend upon the perceived goodness or badness of those elected. The politicians who refused to speak to Sinn Féin members who had been elected by the people were not just attacking a party of which they disapproved, they were attacking a fundamental right of people to choose their own representatives.

Clearly, in creating a new political settlement in Ireland and a modern democracy a lot of hard thinking would have to be done, to which many of the established politicians and churchmen, because of their impoverished ideas of democracy, could apparently contribute little.

It is strange that nowhere, in Ireland or elsewhere, have such issues been discussed. The required condemnation of 'violence' was able to stifle rational discussion about Irish democratic politics.

The idea that one could outlaw politicians who advocated 'violence', that is, the use of military force for political ends, was strange in the circumstances. The Rev. Ian Paisley and the Rev. Martin Smyth could be spoken to, and treated with respect, because they were elected representatives of the people, in spite of the appalling nature of their political programme and the abusiveness of it. Members of British political parties were accepted and treated with respect in Ireland in spite of their truly atrocious record of abusiveness in Ireland and their use of military force in the Malvinas. Members of the British House of Lords, which had on one occasion prevented Home Rule in Ireland and so perpetuated the injustices of the regime, were also treated with respect and spoken to in spite of the fact that they – unlike the ostracised Irish Republicans – had been elected by no one. So the advocacy or use of military means, even of violent means, towards political ends had not been and was not a recognised reason for rejecting other political parties. Sinn Féin was an exception to the rule.

Whatever the reasons for that, the rejection of elected representatives on the grounds that they advocated the use of military force for political ends was spurious, undemocratic and dishonest. Unfortunately, the low standard of political and religious debate in Ireland prevented rational discussion of such matters. Just as the Catholic clergy had elevated obedience to church authorities as the supreme virtue, so Protestant churchmen, and politicians in general, were elevating obedience to the state. Such principles were accepted and no debate about them was necessary. This was unfortunate because here, as in the case of policing and emergency laws, the situation in Northern Ireland could with rational discussion have led to a wider discussion and deeper understanding of possible developments of democracy in other countries as well. We are able now, however, to understand how primitive our ideas of democracy really are: refusal to speak to elected representatives, refusal of the citizens' right to take part in government, enforcement of an unjust system by military and police, the exclusion of poor people from the full use of resources which belong to the whole people, authoritarian structures of church and state, etc. It is without doubt in somebody's interest to keep the level of debate as low as it is in Britain and Ireland, because otherwise we might all realise with a shock how much change we need in our society to make it humane and democratic.

The eagerness of churchmen and politicians to outlaw Sinn Féin is all the more surprising in view of what might be done to other parties in the future. Armed with such a useful and widely accepted precedent any British or Irish government may in the future declare a political party or group 'immoral' and marginalise or destroy it. It did not seem to dawn on people that outlawing an elected party, far from preserving the virtue of society, was a regression into the murk of history. How long is it since either an Irish or a British government enjoyed the luxury of being able to ban elected representatives no matter what the voters say? In the future then would it not be possible for, say, the Workers Party to be outlawed by politicians because its policy on private property is contrary to the Irish Constitution and by churchmen because private property is a matter of divine right? The IRSP could be marginalised because it is Marxist. Anyone who remembers Mr Jack Lynch warning the electorate not many years ago about the left-wing dangers of the very conservative Irish Labour Party will have little doubt that even such a conservative party could well be marginalised again if a powerful party in power so decided. In certain circumstances a party could be marginalised, or worse, because being Catholic it could be declared to be subject to influences from outside the state. Such things have been done before but until recently many of us believed that because we accepted certain democratic principles they were less likely to happen again, principles like the absolute right of people to vote for, and be heard through, elected representatives of their choice. In their anxiety to destroy Sinn Féin politicians and churchmen were cutting a stick which one day might fall on their own backs.

One is reminded of what Thomas More is supposed to have

said when some people wanted to get rid of the constraints of law because they could be a nuisance. 'If you get rid of the law, what protection have you left, however unsatisfactory the law?' One could just as well have said in this situation, however inconvenient the democratic principle, if you remove it which of us shall be safe in the future?

In the Sinn Féin episode it seemed that neither politicians nor churchmen were brave enough to act according to the principles they professed. The faithful were filled with the Holy Spirit and churchmen often told them so, but the same churchmen apparently could not trust the Holy Spirit to help people make political choices without clerical direction. Politicians who talked about the democratic rights of the people did not trust them to vote unless they were firmly told whom they should vote for, and the choice made for them would be enforced by sanctions if needs be. However much we proclaim the heavenly and earthly wisdom of the people, we really do not believe in it. If we did the politicians and churchmen would not have got away with it.

There was probably of course more to the condemnation of Sinn Féin than its support for military action against a government. Most political parties and churches involved in Northern Ireland accept the legitimacy of the use of arms in certain political circumstances. The Official Republicans or Republican Clubs, forerunners of the present Workers Party for example, recognised that while they must try to obtain places in government by non-military means, yet the strength of conservative opposition to them being what it was, they might be deprived of their rights by force; in which case, they believed, recourse to arms would be legitimate. Whether that is the view of the Workers Party is not apparent but if it is not, then there has been a considerable change of attitude since, say, ten years ago. This does not mean that the Workers Party advocates the use of arms as a political tactic. It does mean, however, that it recognises how determined opposition can be even against those who advance through the electoral process, opposition which may eventually have to be confronted with force.

There is no doubt whatever about the Unionist parties' attitude to the use of arms for political ends, nor that of the other British political parties. They have never had any view other than that military force is a legitimate weapon in political struggles. The

Alliance Party has not advocated the use of military means to bring about political change or to enforce a pre-1968 situation in Northern Ireland. It does, however, accept the need for military force to safeguard an internal Northern Ireland settlement if such should be brought about. It might seem that the SDLP does not accept the use of military force for political purposes, but like all political parties involved in Ireland it does. When the 1974 power-sharing executive fell to the accompaniment of the Loyalist workers strike, members of the leadership of the SDLP complained that the British government had not enforced on the streets a settlement they had agreed to at Sunningdale – but they could only have done that by the use of military force, which would have been in this case military enforcement of an unpopular political decision.

If we exclude from discussions those who advocate the use of military force for political reasons we exclude every party in the Northern Ireland conflict.

There has never been any doubt either about the attitude of Christian clergymen to the use of military force. In the 1912-14 period Protestant churchmen in Ireland supported opposition to Home Rule even if such opposition should involve war. It is reported in a book by one of the gun-runners, Colonel Crawford, that from the Larne gun-running of 1914 (*Guns for Ulster*, 1947) one of the first hiding places for the arms was the house of a local Protestant bishop. Catholic churchmen gave post-factum approval to the 1916 Rebellion and subsequent fight against the British government. In 1936-39 the rebellion of General Franco against an elected government in Spain was hailed as a crusade for Christ. The Hungarian revolt in 1956 was praised by churchmen, its refugees and participants hailed as victims and heroes. The Christians have accepted many revolutions and believe that they were justified in doing so. They refuse to accept the legitimacy of the Republican revolution in Northern Ireland not because they are against revolutions in general but because they are against this one. They have never been called upon to explain, in the light of their history, exactly why.

That there is an element of class distinction somewhere is quite likely. Churchmen in Northern Ireland as elsewhere have traditionally believed that religious leadership should come from the clergy and political leadership from the upper and middle

classes. Among Catholics the change brought about by the Second
Vatican Council allowed lay people to take a greater part in church
affairs, but major decisions were still to be made by the clergy.
Among Protestants there are more democratic forms of church
government but in practice lay people are seldom seen or heard
as spokespersons for the Protestant churches; clerics are still the
leaders in church affairs. In political and social life the same kind
of class principles apply as in the churches.

Many people still believe that the big house is more able to
produce political and social leaders than the council house. The
Catholic church has a definite policy on the matter: in 1984
Bishop Cathal Daly of Belfast expressed disappointment at the
failure of the Catholic middle class in Northern Ireland to take an
effective part in politics, 'because it is from the middle classes that
leadership can be expected to come'. For Protestants it is
traditionally the gentry and the Orange Order who are to supply
the leaders. The tension between Rev. Paisley and Rev. Martin
Smyth, both Loyalist, both Protestant, is to a great degree based
upon the fear, or the hope, that leadership may pass from the
gentry and higher business classes to the lower middle classes on
whom Paisley largely depends. In our anxiety to interpret the
Northern Ireland situation as one of conflict between Catholics
and Protestants as such, we do not take notice of the class conflict
which exists within and between various groups in the conflict.
It is interesting to note that of the prime ministers of Northern
Ireland, Lord Craigavon (1921-1940) and Lord Brookeborough
(1943-1963) held office for about twenty years each while J. M.
Andrews, a merchant, was able to held office for only a few years
(1940-1943). Towards the end to the Stormont regime O'Neill
(1963-1969) was followed by his kinsman Chichester-Clark
(1969-1972), both gentry. When the premiership was taken by
Faulkner, a merchant (1971-1972) Stormont fell for good. It was
like the twilight of the gods. Either the gentry ruled or there was
no Stormont. After the fall of Stormont in 1972 if the gentry were
to rule they would do so from the House of Lords. And they do.
A tactical retreat to a new position.

In such a class-conscious society it is natural that a party like
Sinn Féin is less than acceptable. The old Nationalist Party was
clericalist – it was normal for a local parish priest to preside over
Nationalist meetings to choose election candidates – and class

conscious. Some of the most articulate opponents of the introduction of the welfare state in the North of Ireland were Nationalists; they were never a working class party and had no intention of ever becoming one. When the Social Democratic and Labour Party was born in 1970 one of the unstated aims was to make sure that the old clericalism did not attach itself to the new party. One of the effects of the emergence of Sinn Féin was that the SDLP was to some extent flung into the arms of the clergy who supported them against Sinn Féin, thus leaving the way open again for some clerical influence over the party, an influence which may prove significant in the future. A party like Sinn Féin which was reborn out of the conflicts in the poorest parts of Northern Ireland and proclaims the need for a Socialist Republic is hardly likely to be acceptable in a society in which class is so important to religious and political leaders.

Which of all these factors is the most important in creating the widespread condemnation and marginalising of Sinn Féin is impossible to say – its origins, its social class, its Socialism, its Republicanism, its support of the use of arms. It may well be that the last of these although the most often proclaimed is in reality the one that counts least among many of the condemners.

6

Britain's Real Purpose in Ireland

Why does the British government wish to keep a foothold in Ireland?

The reasons given for British occupation of part of Ireland have varied over the years. For example, in the 1920s the stated purpose was to protect the interests of Irish Protestants. But when the crisis of 1969 came and Catholics came under attack the world was told that the British troops were being sent in, in force, in order to protect the Catholics; the troops were there to keep the peace between two factions.

Within a year, however, the scene had changed and what was described as the honeymoon period of Catholic and British army tolerance was over. Now the world was told that the purpose of the British troops in Ireland was to fight the IRA. This remained the message for some years.

But fighting the IRA, however important it seemed at home, was not necessarily the best message for international consumption. It was clear by the end of the 1970s that while the Americans might be interested in helping their British allies in every way possible it was not good American policy to intervene in a fight which was purely internal. In a sense the British government by insisting that the Northern Ireland situation was an internal United Kingdom one had distanced the Americans from their cause, because American policy did not favour, in theory at any rate, American intervention where 'terrorism' was being used internally.

Since the beginning of the 1980s, therefore, we notice that the stated purpose of British military occupation of Northern Ireland has been 'to combat international terrorism'. As the American government is committed, it says, to combating international terrorism this formula ensures American sympathy and defuses any possible American domestic objections to being allied to

Britain against Irish dissidents.

The new explanation of what Britain was doing in Ireland had the bonus that in other European countries the same preoccupation with international terrorism was evident. The British government could not be expected to elicit international sympathy and support by saying that its troops were in Ireland to protect Protestants, or Catholics, or even indeed to fight the IRA – the European Community did not much care about any of these causes. But it did care about 'international terrorism', and so this is the explanation of the British presence in Ireland which has been most current during the last five years. It is constantly reiterated, and unfortunately has never been questioned in Ireland.

That is to say, the explanations given abroad of Britain's presence in Ireland have always had more to do with the needs of international propaganda than with the realities of the matter. The explanation which was most acceptable abroad was the one that was put forward. Yet even the fight against 'international terrorism' was not sufficient. As the need to counter adverse propaganda in America increased, the British government began, about the beginning of this decade, to say that the purpose of their troops in Ireland was to prevent 'another Cuba' on her own doorstep. Significantly, it was a period of intense fear in the United States of the emergence of Socialist states on their own periphery – Nicaragua and Cuba were symbols of encirclement which the Americans very much feared. The Americans would, therefore, be sure to understand not only Britain's fight against 'international terror' but also her desire to protect herself – and Europe – against the possibility of a European Cuba.

The evolution of British explanations of what it is doing in Ireland is interesting in itself. One explanation, of course, had shaded into another as time went on, and all the explanations contrast strongly with the generally held historical view that Britain's purpose in Ireland in previous centuries was to provide itself with military bases and to ensure that a viable Irish economy would never be created.

But however interesting it may be in itself, far more interesting is the question of Britain's real motives in staying in Ireland. If the explanation given to the world has changed five or six times in the space of sixteen years, what explanation will be given to the world in two years time, or ten? Given the pattern of the past that will depend upon the needs of British propaganda abroad. It need have little to do with the realities of the situation in Ireland or in Britain.

The real reasons have simply not been given, and for some reason, not easy to understand, have never been demanded by successive Irish governments.

It is also strange that the role of Britain as peace-keeper between warring factions is still accepted in Ireland itself. Dr O'Brien, a writer of Irish origins, accepts the bloodbath theory which has been put forward by Unionists in general, namely that in the event of British withdrawal from Ireland there would be a civil war, disastrous and extremely bloody, which would result in the defeat of those who broadly speaking could be called 'Nationalists'. Mr Napier, past leader of the Alliance Party has warned of a 'conflagration from Ballycastle (Co. Antrim) to Cork' if British withdrawal takes place. The Rev. Paisley and other Protestant leaders have given similar warnings. The most common reaction to this kind of threat in Ireland is to believe it. This reinforces the belief that the British army is truly a peace-keeping force which the people cannot do without. That is to say, while the main thrust of British explanations abroad is that it is fighting international terrorism, their message in Ireland is that they are protecting the Irish from killing each other.

There is no need here to weigh up the validity of the bloodbath or any other theory. It should be open to rational discussion by commentators, not simply reiteration by politicians. It is either valid or it is not, and after all it is those who might be expected to fight such a civil war who should know, and they have not been asked how precisely they expect to do it and how exactly they hope to win it. The substitution of threats for analysis has been one of the more unfortunate features of the Irish situation especially in its modern phase.

If the general public are satisfied in America and Europe with the 'fight against international terrorism' theory and those at home are satisfied with 'the bloodbath' theory no further explanations are needed. But one has to ask why it is that while historians accept that military and economic needs were the reasons for Britain's presence in Ireland in the past politicians and commentators today cannot even consider that the same is true now? Why is it that the explanation of what happened in the last century is not acceptable as the explanation of what is happening today? Perhaps academics can be objective about Britain's policies towards Ireland in the eighteenth and nineteenth centuries, yet find it more difficult or less expedient to be objective about her policies towards us now. If her reasons for staying in Ireland are economic and military, let us say so. And if this throws into question the whole concept of international terrorism as applied to Ireland, or of international terrorism in general, so be it. Politics should be about facts not explanations. And as for the religious people, it is enough to remember that it is the truth – not the government information sheets – that will set you free.

By accepting Britain's rôle in Ireland as a peace-keeper we are forced to agree with politicians who say that the British government would leave Ireland if it could. This is the Irish modern equivalent of the white man's burden, a concept dismissed in most places today with wry amusement at best and, at worst, execration. Although it is often stated that the British government wishes to leave Ireland no proof has ever been brought forward to prove that it does. At the 1972 Oxford conference mentioned earlier it was stated, but no proof was given. Indeed proof to the contrary was given by the events of Bloody Sunday in Derry. When an Irish politician says that the British government wishes to get out, he will never adduce proof of it. He will probably say, as Dr Garret FitzGerald has said, that he knows high-ranking members of the British establishment – the kind whom we listened to near Oxford in 1972 doubtless – and this is what they say. The British government is not prepared to make any statement suggesting any such thing in public, and the idea that it wishes to be disengaged from Ireland sounds rather like the kind of remark one would throw at one's Irish friends in a London club and laugh about afterwards. All the evidence is that Britain wishes to remain in Ireland. Therefore, it is futile to think of reaching a settlement, or of removing the British government, until we know the exact reason, not the stated reason for it wishing to stay.

The idea of the British government as a disinterested peace-keeper has miraculously survived in spite of injustice, torture, maladministration, military aggression at home and militarist adventures abroad. It would seem that the idea persists because so many Irish politicians and churchmen want it to.

During the past few years, however, there has been an increasing tendency to analyse Britain's rôle in Ireland more rigorously. This is being done in the smaller, perhaps radical, groups in Ireland rather than in the larger parties. The smaller groups discuss economic and military reasons, that is, Britain's self-interest, while the larger parties generally talk about obligations which Britain has towards Ireland – Britain being a so-called friendly nation. The idea of Britain as a friendly nation, in view of the injustice, ridicule and torture it has offered to our citizens is bizarre. It would be unacceptable in any other nation in Europe. Some special, irrational relationship between Ireland and Britain, however, seems to demand that the notion of Britain as an unfriendly nation cannot be entertained. The time has come for thinking of this kind to be revised. Irish people need to be very clear when charity sours into servility.

In Britain there is an increasing awareness now of the realities of the Irish situation partly because of events in Britain itself. The recent miners' strike caused some politicisation roughly similar to that of Northern Ireland Catholics in the years 1966-1983 when they became more and more aware of the true nature of the regime under which they lived and the enormous apparatus of counter attack it was prepared to use against those who opposed it. By a strange irony the British miners, from whose numbers the most repressive of British Secretaries had come, Roy Mason, found themselves in Ireland during their own time of trouble asking for help from Irish people. That such help was given without anyone recalling the miners' gift to Ireland in the shape of Mason is a tribute to Irish people who received the miners and subscribed to their strike fund. It is bad politics, however good it may be for the soul, to hand over anything without getting something in return. The attitude of many Irish people towards the miners was interesting from this point of view. Help was given to the miners but Irish people never asked, or got, any assurance that in return the miners would insist that the British government send over no more people of Mason's calibre. Given another Labour government in Britain there is no reason to believe it would not.

We have to look carefully at British statements of policy regarding Ireland. The armed Republican movement's policy has been for many years that given a declaration by the British government to withdraw – not actual withdrawal but a declaration of intent to withdraw – the war in Ireland against the British government will end. The declaration of intent has never been given. Instead, the government says that it will stay as long as a majority wish it to stay; many people seem to take for granted that there is a corollary to this, namely that if a majority in the North of Ireland wish the British government to depart it will do so. That is not so. No such declaration has ever been made by the British government. It has made statements, for example, that in the event of a majority of this kind emerging in Northern Ireland the British government will 'facilitate' new arrangements which will accommodate the wishes of this new majority. But the myth persists that when the British government says it will remain in Ireland as long as a majority in the six Ulster counties wish it to, it means also that it will depart when a majority there wishes it to depart. There is no evidence of any such intention but the politicians allow the people to believe there is.

Parallel to the refusal of the British government to state its real reasons for staying in Ireland is the Irish politicians' refusal to state the reasons for wanting it to stay. A number of reasons are given: fear of a bloodbath, fear of sectarian warfare, need to negotiate rather than force political settlement, respect for the Unionist Irish. In face of the treatment they have received at the hands of the British administration it comes as a shock to many people in the North to realise that Irish politicians have at times specifically asked the British government to remain rather than demanded that it leaves at the first possible opportunity. One can accept that the desire to keep the British government in place is due to economic reasons just as the British policy in Ireland is due to economic reasons, among others. But if so, the Irish government should say so. It is just as unbecoming that the Irish government should give false guarantees to the Nationalists as that the British government should give them to the Unionists. The guarantees of neither government will survive in face of new economic, political or military necessities experienced by Britain.

To put it brutally, however, the Nationalists in the North are just as likely to be betrayed by Irish politicians as both they and the Unionists are by the British. There are Unionists and Nationalists in the North who believe with good reason that by 1985 the process of betrayal was well under way.

7

The Military Clergymen

The belief that in certain political circumstance the use of military force is justified is held in Northern Ireland not only by armed Republicans but by all the political parties and churches. There are pacifists in Ireland, some of whom have suffered for their pacifism, whether it was protesting against the Second World War outside Belfast City Hall in 1939, or protesting right up to the present day outside Bishopscourt, Co. Down, the British Air Force base. In these and other protests pacifists have been derided and sometimes physically beaten. They have conducted a peaceful and dignified campaign against war. But they never persuaded political parties or churchmen to give up the idea that military force is moral and indispensible; or even to stop accepting military force as not only the lesser of two evils but even as a good in itself.

Recruitment to the military is encouraged in Christian based schools in Northern Ireland just as it is elsewhere. The induction into the use of arms occurs as early as the first grades in primary schools. Schools and universities have their officer induction and training centres. Even the Christian uniformed associations have a military ethos, with military titles, drilling etc. It is not accidental that many Christian associations are run on military lines. Boys' Scouts, Boys' Brigade – even the names are evocative of military action – the Salvation Army with its military titles, colonel, major etc., even the Legion of Mary, drawn up like an army in battle array, to quote the handbook written by its founder Frank Duff, a most peaceful man. This is not the place to discuss fully the connections between Christians and the military. They are long standing, deep and possibly irreversible. The Christians have a religious-military culture. The point is made here in order to underline one of the aspects of the Northern Ireland situation, that is, the involvement of the Christians, including clergymen, in military associations. Some Christian clergymen are part-time

soldiers in the Ulster Defence Regiment and the British army
territorials. Some are Royal Navy reservists. Others are members
of unofficial armed bodies. It is likely that if we were to exclude
all Protestant clergymen who are members of either armed
organisations or secret societies (the Masons, Orange and Black
orders, etc.) there would be only a minority left.

Among Catholic clergy the situation is different, not because
Catholic clergymen always avoid either secret societies or armed
forces, but because there are not many secret societies in the
North of Ireland which would welcome them or armed groups
which they would want to join or in which they would be
welcomed. There are very few Catholic clergymen members of
the British armed forces; membership of unofficial armed forces
is probably nil.

Churchmen in Ireland do not criticise armed forces as such.
When they criticise the police or military they criticise what they
see as the excesses of the forces, not the forces themselves or their
presence in the Irish situation. For example, when Cardinal
Conway was induced by some clergy to protest to the British
government about the tortures which interned men were
subjected to in 1971 he did not protest against internment as such
– although it was assumed by many people that he did – or against
the presence of the British military in Ireland. Politicians in the
South of Ireland did not reject internment as such or the presence
of the British army as such, but the excesses committed on the
occasion of internment or at times by the troops.

The difference between the approach of Cardinal Conway and
that of Cardinal Ó Fiaich is that the latter is willing to call for the
removal not only of the abuses but the cause of the abuses as well.
This is not new, although it is not convenient for the press in
Ireland or Britain to note this fact. It is a return to the attitude
of Catholic bishops in the 1920 period who protested against
partition as unnatural and of Bishop Daniel Mageean in
particular, who as Bishop of Down and Connor protested against
the presence of the British troops and for many years refused even
to appoint a chaplain for them. But even those who opposed the
presence of British troops in Ireland did so not because they
disapproved of the military as such. It was because they
disapproved of a certain kind of force in a certain place. Church
of Ireland bishops visit Irish army barracks on the Southern side

of the border, the Cardinal inspects a military guard of honour, the Pope was transported in Ireland in an army helicopter and lunched with the Minister for Defence (not the Minister responsible for social welfare); these things are accepted as natural and acceptable in Ireland. Not surprisingly many clergymen in the North are even more closely linked with the use of arms in their situation.

Clergymen will in general accuse the forces, if at all, of over-reaction, or recklessness, or, more frequently, of giving propaganda to the IRA. Similarly, they will say for example, not that strip-searching of women prisoners should be abolished but that is should be done only for unavoidable security reasons or with dignity. The number of clergy, who advocate the abolition of the present military presence in the North, the disbandment of certain forces like the UDR and the cessation of degrading practices like internment and strip-searching altogether is very small.

It is impossible to say how many clergymen in Northern Ireland are engaged in armed groups. Church leaders are unwilling to say for obvious reasons. It can be said, however, that the number is substantial. This need not come as a surprise to anyone, although the lack of comment about it is surprising in view of the constant questions which men like Cardinal Ó Fiaich have to answer about Catholic clerical attitudes to Republican military campaigns.

There is a strong tradition of armed clergymen which goes back far into Christian history. In Ireland and in continental Europe the pages of history are dotted with the exploits of soldier bishops, fighting abbots, warring monasteries, religious orders devoted to fighting the Turk.

Present day Northern Ireland is part of a long Christian tradition, a warlike tradition. If the Christians there were content just to give ritual expression to this tradition all would be well. After all, they do us a service when as Knights of Malta or of St Lazarus they are present at almost every upheavel in the streets. And they and their ceremonies can be quite colourful. But they are not content with ritual. The Orange Order is not just a ritualistic order, it is a religious-military order on active service. In 1985 the message of the religious Orange Order was explicit and clear: it was prepared to take up arms if necessary. It did not seem to occur to anyone listening to this clear message that for a religious order, led by a clergyman, Martin Smyth, and supported in worship by hundreds of other clergymen, to declare itself ready to take up arms was strange, worthy of comment and a dangerous reversion to the middle ages. Nobody commented on the anomaly. The enormity of such a situation can be understood if one imagines say the Knights of Columbanus or Opus Dei making a similar declaration of intent to take up arms for political purposes. People would notice. Perhaps one can get so used to armed clergymen that like Chesterton's waiter one does not notice them any more.

Many Christians do not look upon involvement in arms, even by clergymen, as a disgrace. On the contrary, they accept it as normal and with good reason. The Christians' reverence for soldiering can be traced back not, as some Christian pacifists like to believe to the post-Constantine era but to the very beginnings of Christianity. There never was a pacifist Christian church. There were Christian pacifists but the Christians as a body never, even from the beginning, had a pacifist theology. If they want to invoke one now they will have to create one. The Christian warriors of present day Northern Ireland are very much like the first of their kind.

It is a curious fact, which we always overlook, that Jesus is never reported in the Gospel as saying that soldiers must give up soldiering in order to become his followers. Rich people were told to part with their wealth, tax collectors to give away their excess profits, the 'dead' were to be left to bury their dead; fishermen to leave their nets and others were to leave their jobs to become Jesus' followers. But on no occasion did Jesus commend or suggest to a soldier to give up his soldiering. If he had wanted to do so there were occasions when he could suitably have done so. Even John the Baptist with all his talk of radical changes – the axe being laid to the roots of the tree – did not ask soldiers to give up soldiering. They were to be content with their pay and not beat people. That is, wherever changes were to come about in Christian times the abolition of soldiering was not necessarily to be one of them.

It is true that if everyone were to do what Jesus commanded and lovingly turn the other cheek, soldiering would become unnecessary and wither away. But the same is true of wealth, yet while Jesus told people they could with difficulty enter the Kingdom with wealth he made no comment about entering the

Kingdom with a sword. If Jesus had availed of his opportunities to ask people to abandon soldiering the Christians would have faced the world with the pacifist theology it desperately needs. As it happened, the Christians after two thousand years still do not know whether they are pacifists or not; and most of them think they probably are not.

Many Christians for whom Paul is a model of discipline find no difficulty in accepting military Christianity. Paul after all expressed great admiration for the discipline of the Roman soldiers and even drew from the life of soldiers a lesson for the behaviour of Christian preachers! The pacifist may well grieve that Paul did not give the lesson the other way about.

The Christians of those early times and up to 200 AD believed much as we do now about the need for military intervention in our affairs. The military forces of the Roman army stood between the Christian citizens and the barbarians. The emperor had a right to his forces because he had a divine right to rule, military force was the lesser of two evils. The same arguments are being used by the Christians in Northern Ireland today about the British army.

Rev. Donald Gillies, a Presbyterian clergyman, made the matter clear some years ago when he said that so far from Christian contact and friendship with others creating peace, the community needed a framework of law and order to be imposed – by force if necessary – so that Christians could exercise charity towards each other. Although most would not state the matter so explicitly, his is a generally held view among the Christians in Ireland. If one understands this one understands the apparent anomaly of Christians professing to love each other while at the same time calling for severe military and police action against their fellow citizens. What they are saying is not the result of some eccentricity which afflicts Irish Christians, it is the logical result of the philosophy they have, a philosophy accurately expressed by Rev. Donald Gillies. Military and police impose law and order, and the Christians have the ambiance in which they can love one another.

It could be said in response to this that Christians should create peace through their love for each other and as taught by the psalmist should not rely on 'horses and chariots', or tanks and guns. There have been many suggestions that the armed Republicans should lay down their guns, or that the British military should depart, that the Loyalists should cease their armed action. What has seldom if ever been suggested is that the whole Northern Ireland situation should, by a careful and patient process of negotiation, be completely demilitarised.

The Christians do not as a body approve of demilitarisation. In such a situation where churchmen, who have enormous influence, have such sympathy for the military it is not surprising that while, on the one hand, Christian clergymen invoke the help of the military, the military also use the clergy. One of the most revealing episodes of the British campaign in Northern Ireland was their use of army chaplains to gather information.

In the north of Ireland from 1969 onwards it was known that some army chaplains took part in army patrols. From time to time a chaplain would appear in a parochial house on friendly visits, but armed. Little notice was taken because in other countries as well chaplains to the forces created similar problems. A study of Royal Air Force chaplains for instance (*Chaplains in the RAF*, Gorden C. Zahn, 1969) showed that they often acted more as military personnel than as priests. But notice had to be taken when it was observed that some British army chaplains who in the early 1970s had free entry into people's homes – they were clergymen and as such were welcomed – were found to be asking questions which residents of one West Belfast district complained 'were more the kind of questions the police or army officers would be asking'. In other parts of Northern Ireland some army chaplains used their position to confront school teachers with photographs of Republicans, asking who or where they might be. It soon became clear that some army chaplains were gathering information and the church authorities did not deny that this had happened. The problem facing local clergy in many places where it happened was clear: their relationship with people depended upon confidentiality. If the people could not trust them to keep their confidence they might as well pack up and leave. Now the army chaplains were threatening this confidential relationship.

The discovery of this operation, which had been going on for a long time, led to private and public recrimination between some of the clergy as well as between local clergy and army chaplains. It was a startling revelation of how far the army authorities were prepared to go in order to collect intelligence and of how far clergymen in the army were prepared to go to help them. It was also shown by these incidents that in such operations the local church authorities would either support the military, condone what was being done, or remain silent. When one discusses the relationships between churchmen and others in situations like that of Northern Ireland one must take into account how far some churchmen have been prepared to go to support the institutions of the state, even the army.

One of the army chaplains most closely involved in this kind of operation in Belfast was Father Gerry Weston, who was later killed by a bomb said to have been placed by the Official IRA at the barracks in Aldershot. There is no indication that his death had anything to do however with his intelligence gathering in Belfast. That this priest did what he did voluntarily was apparent during the discussions which occurred after the discovery of what was happening. I met a senior army chaplain, also a Catholic priest, and asked him bluntly 'whether Gerry Weston had done what he did because he wanted to or because he had been persuaded by the army.' Without hesitation the man replied, 'I think he was pressured by the army'.

It could be argued that clergymen of all people must appreciate that everyone has a soul to save and therefore their ministry must be to soldiers as well as to everyone else. But to save the soul of a grocer you do not have to sell beans. It could equally be argued that clergymen should be wary of giving any special recognition to soldiers and that whatever else he does he should not join them. However, in the North of Ireland the Christians solved questions like these by adherence to military ideals, military discipline and at times even military actions, all of which deserve scrutiny. The closeness of the Christians to the military in any situation, not only that of the North of Ireland, is such that one may well wonder whether they should, as they are, be accorded unquestioningly the title of men of peace. Some of them are unmistakably men of war.

Not all clergymen who have been connected with armed forces remain so. Monsignor Bruce Kent who served with the British armed forces – not in Ireland – became the leader of the Campaign for Nuclear Disarmament and a pacifist. The Rev. Ray Davey, founder of Corrymeela Reconciliation Centre, served with the British forces in North Africa. Dr Butler, one time Anglican Bishop in Belfast and one of its foremost workers for reconciliation, had been a member of the British armed forces; Father Seán Curran, one time director of the Glencree Reconciliation Centre, was a member of the Irish armed forces, as was Father McGreil who is now also a pacifist. The same road which led them from the armed forces to pacifism or to work for reconciliation led Peter Emerson, a Belfast based pacifist (not a cleric though) from the British armed forces to sit-down protests outside RAF bases in County Down and anti-war protests elsewhere. The presence of people of this kind within peace and reconciliation movements of this kind is interesting.

People are led into armed groups and out again, some to become pacifists, some not. It happens to clergy from time to time and of those who make such a journey from armed action to non-military action some become the most notable of peace workers. This fact should have warned us not to make too facile judgements about others who make a similar journey.

There is a myth that once a person becomes a member of an armed group, Loyalist or Republican, he cannot leave it. This is not true. There is hardly a greater nuisance to an armed group than a reluctant fighter and in any case a half-hearted member of an armed organisation is a security risk whom armed groups will avoid if they can. It is probably easier to stop serving in a Republican or Loyalist military group than it is to stop serving in the British army – at least you don't have to buy yourself out.

Politicians – and therefore clergymen – are unwilling to believe that if a citizen has once borne arms against the government he can ever act politically in any other way in the future. (Incidentally, politicians are more ready to attribute transition from military to non-military politics to Loyalist than to Republican groups. A minister of the government was present at the opening of a UDA [Ulster Defence Association] club and danced with some of its members. One could not envisage a government minister dancing with members of a newly-opened Sinn Féin club.) But passage from armed to non-armed political activity can and does happen, and one can consider it normal. Just as members of the British forces may make a political journey from military to non-military activity so can the private citizen. When, therefore, we hear of a citizen doing so we ought not to dismiss him as a fake. When we hear of organisations creating a non-military campaign where before they were engaged only in a military one, we should not dismiss this either, unless we wish to pretend that such things were never done honestly. We might just as well contend that all the people who have moved from the state military forces to private pacifism or reconciliation are fakes too.

It is unfortunately true that such thinking is not welcome among either politicians or churchmen in Ireland. I watched with dismay how those who had said, 'If only the Republicans would turn to the voting booth, then things would be different', turned on them when they did so and refused them either the normal rights of elected representatives or the courtesies the people who voted for them were entitled to expect.

Generally political parties could be expected to look after their own interests but churchmen of all people should have acted differently and at least accepted all political parties at their own evaluation. Those who, in the pulpits, proclaimed that everyone could change now proclaimed with even greater fervour that their political opponents could never change.

The transition from military to non-military activity is something which can be achieved in any case only slowly, patiently and with great delicacy. And there must be sufficient gains to enable military politicians to make the transition. If the gains are in the direction of justice then no one need have any fears about what is happening. It is never an immoral surrender to anyone to give justice to people.

The whole question of the Christians' contribution or failure to contribute to the demilitarisation of Northern Ireland should be examined, for it is a dark question indeed. That they have contributed to militarisation is beyond doubt, that they have the capacity to help demilitarise by negotiation is probably true if they so desire.

The sad truth seems to be that they do not so desire. Many clergymen want the war to continue until it is assured that Republicans will have no say whatever in the running of whatever state emerges from the war. Others want the war to stop but can envisage only military means to stop it. Others want the destruction of the Republicans by some means or other. There has hardly been, however, a single recorded instance of clergymen in Ireland saying that the right thing to do is sit around a table with the military parties and discuss whether the war can be ended without dishonour to anybody. If the Christian clergy cannot take the first step towards this, then they can have no valid complaint if others cannot do it either. After all, the clergymen proclaim a gospel which says: 'If your brother does something wrong go and have it out with him alone, between your two selves. If he listens to you, you have won back your brother. If he does not listen, take one or two others along with you. . . If he refuses to listen to these. . .' (Matt. 18:15ff)

Sometimes it is said that Christians in Northern Ireland have an ambivalent attitude to 'violence', meaning military political activity by citizens or by governments. Their attitude in most cases is not ambivalent, it is quite firmly in favour of the use of military force when necessary. Their commitment to the use of arms has indeed made the Christians one of the most powerful and successfully warlike people of the past two thousand years. Ambivalence is not an obviously suitable word to describe that kind of record.

The word does however make sense if you place side by side with this successful militarism the professed desire of the Christians to regulate their affairs by love and forgiveness. Thus Christians sway uncertainly from one ideal to the other, from military action to non-military, from war to peace, from law and order to a kind of lovable chaos. They never, however, all fall into pacifism at the same time.

We cannot expect them to do so, because they would have to leave behind them a vast history in which militarism and Christianity have been closely intertwined. They would have to change their politics for today and this itself would bring dramatic and welcome changes in the political scene in Northern Ireland and elsewhere. We cannot, after so many disappointments, expect them now to take a mighty leap away from the attitudes of the past and present into a new pacifist political and theological world. For Christians there is always a limit to the foolishness of the cross. No adequate theology exists in any of the Christian groups which would enable them to become pacifists in practice even if in theory they accepted that they should. There are no signs of them doing that anyway. They are unwilling to become the weak ones, who, they say themselves, overcome the strong. They still trust – against scriptural advice – in the modern equivalent of horses and chariots for their earthly safety.

But the real disappointment of anyone watching the Christians at work or at war in the North of Ireland is the almost complete absence of generous gestures by one Christian group to another.

It is the absence of Christian generosity more than the presence of Christian arms that hurts most deeply.

8

The Ecumenical Clergymen

It would be wrong to think of Northern Ireland as a place where clerical bigots and clerical soldiers flourish and clerics of no other kind exist. True, they have an inordinate influence, but there are other clergymen who are important too.

In the 1960s there was an unprecedented coming together of Christians, including Protestant and Catholic clergy. It was part of the movement in which Nationalists and Unionists, Catholics and Protestants were uniting in an effort to bring about political and religious reconciliation. The efforts were severely damaged by the rise of Paisley and the weakness of other Christians, and by the end of the decade the houses were burning again. But this movement should be recognised nevertheless.

The Second Vatican Council which took place at the beginning of the 1960s helped, but was not responsible for, this movement. It helped because it was an opening up of the Catholic church to the world. But it was not responsible for the movement of Catholics and Protestants towards each other; that would probably have happened anyway. The Second Vatican Council, indeed, probably did not initiate any movements among Christians. From the many fresh ideas which Christians were experimenting with in the previous two decades the Council selected some for approval, others it rejected, without condemning any. But in doing so it established a norm to which we have been looking back ever since. That is to say, after the Council it was no longer acceptable to create or experiment with new ideas; everything had to be referred back to the Vatican Council. Those who tried to create new Christian thinking by looking forward to the needs of the future rather than backwards to the dictates of the past soon found that they were now bound by a set of documents which even if they were not as restrictive as Trent would be just as authoritative. Catholic Christians, in

other words, would still have to look *back* in order to validate
their fresh ideas. Looking *forward*, which had been in fashion
before the Vatican Council, would not be in fashion any more.
Pope John, while enjoying a reputation for being progressive had
forced Catholic thinkers once more to subject themselves to a
norm which was, as always, in the past.

Catholic thinkers would have to realise that 'progressive'
thinking, that is, creating a Christian ideology according to what
they saw as the needs of the future, was not approved. Just as
before, they would now have to refer back to an approved norm,
the Second Vatican Council, more liberal than before, but as
constraining in many ways as any previous normative councils
had been. The Council did not create progressive or reconciliating
movements. It may well indeed have inhibited them.

In the North of Ireland it is hardly to be expected that the
Second Vatican Council made a great deal of difference in the
1960s. For one thing the Catholic church authorities wished to
minimise its effect, and for another the Protestants did not quite
understand what it was all about. Naturally, different people
interpreted such events according to how they believed they
would affect their own interests. But there were signs that many
people wanted a new deal in both politics and religion. The signs
had been there before the Council was heard of. This was only to
be expected. During the Second World War the German
occupation of European countries had shown people that many of
their disagreements were futile. Protestants, Catholics, Jews,
Communists, agnostics, found themselves engaged in the same
war, sharing prison and wondering why so many petty differences
should have separated them in the past. In France and Holland
particularly the importance of religious differences seemed to
grow less as shared experience grew. There was some hope that
in the North of Ireland the shared unhappy experience not only
of the war years but of life as it had unhappily been in the area,
would help bring people together also. They had after all come
face to face with greater conflict and causes than their own.

The movement of Catholics and Protestants towards each other
after the Second World War was slow to develop. The Orange
Order, which had during the war been less active publicly, began
to re-emerge. Paisley was conducting his small but locally effective
campaign against Romanism, but open bigotry had become less

respectable. The beginning of the 1960s was an interesting and hopeful time in Northern Ireland. The arrival of a new Catholic bishop in Belfast in 1962, the appointment in 1963 of a new Catholic Archbishop of Armagh, who was knowledgeable and intelligent, the emergence of a policy of contact and co-operation between North and South made many people in the North more optimistic than they had ever been. As time went on in the early part of the 1960s the movement, which had been visible even ten years earlier, developed. It became possible, then fashionable, for groups to invite mixed gatherings of Unionists and Nationalists, Protestants and Catholics, 'Southern' and 'Northern' speakers, on to their platforms. There was a movement towards reconciliation.

Sometimes the importance given to small events in this context shows the pathetic childishness of the thinking that lay behind it. The fact that the Unionist City Council in Belfast lowered the union jack as a mark of respect on the death of Pope John XXIII was an example (1963). It was treated as an event of national importance. It was assumed then by many people that the Northern Protestants had been converted to a new view of the Papacy, or at least of the Pope, by the pleasant and humane personality of John. But the Northern Protestants knew practically nothing about John. It is just as likely that the Northern Protestants, having by themselves arrived at the point where they knew they needed some kind of reconciliation with Catholics, found that the death of John gave them the opportunity to show some courtesy on an occasion when it would really count. The movement towards understanding was already there and John, with his Second Vatican Council, which was interpreted generally as progressive, had helped to reassure Protestants that their attempts to create a new deal were worthwhile.

One could argue about the reasons why Protestant Unionists wanted such a new deal at all. There is no doubt that Prime Minister O'Neill, with his inherited and cultivated contempt for Catholics believed that, like it or not, Catholic co-operation was needed for the survival of the state. Faulkner, who was probably not a bigot but like other politicians pretended to be one, knew that the survival of the state depended upon Catholic consent. In the movement towards reconciliation a lot of things had to be overlooked, for example, the principle that one who is a bigot and shows it is less despicable than one who pretends to be a bigot for money or power. There was no pretence with Paisley who was apparently unable to see that in the new climate changes were required and that anti-Catholicism alone was going to do more political harm than good. Northern Ireland was dividing itself into a number of camps: those who believed that a new deal must be done for political and economic reasons, those who believed that a new deal should be done for religious and humane reasons, and those who believed that no deal need be done and the old antagonisms should be kept alive. One could not afford to distinguish too severely between the first and second of these because after all, any kind of reconciliation was better than none. Indeed one could never know to which camp an ecumenist or pluralist belonged.

The hopeful thing about the 1960s was that there were Christian clergymen with a more open and generous view of their Catholic fellow citizens than had been seen before. They were men with inquiring minds who wanted for whatever reason new approaches to religious, social and political matters. It would be impossible, and ungenerous, to pretend that any of us knew them all. At the risk of appearing to single out some as against others, I can mention Presbyterian leaders like the late Dr James Haire, Dr Alfie Martin, Dr Patterson; among the Methodists Rev. Eric Gallagher, Rev. Sidney Callaghan; among the Church of Ireland clergymen, Archbishop George Simms, Canon Eric Elliott, Bishop Arthur Butler, Bishop Anthony Hanson, Rev. Brian Harvey. I cannot know or name them all but there were enough generous clergymen to help create a movement which was both open and generous. Among the Catholic clergy also there were men who wanted a new approach to Protestant thinking and to Protestants. But like their Protestant colleagues they were diffident and over cautious. These clergymen during the 1960s helped to create a climate in Northern Ireland suitable for a charitable exchange of views and for the creation of religiously rich friendships among Christians. The structure of the churches made it unlikely that women would be able to contribute to the movement as much as they were entitled and able to do. Like politics, religious events in Northern Ireland were controlled largely by men.

Unfortunately, such clergymen in spite of their open and generous approach to each other did not have an adequate theology to enable them to achieve a new kind of Christian life, nor did they have the ability to create one.

The Catholic church authorities did not accept that ecumenism meant Christians and others coming together for a free sharing of ideas. It meant carefully monitored discussions which would be attended by carefully chosen clergymen, in meetings which could not but lack spontaniety and adventurousness. This kind of ecumenism, for which the norms were set in Belfast by men like Bishop Philbin, and also by intelligent and informed churchmen like William Conway in Armagh, became the standard for the Ballymascanlon talks and other ecumenical meetings which have been taking place since then between church leaders. Ecumenism was, it seemed, a meeting of experts to discuss common ground on which the faithful could walk without danger. The possibility of the faithful joyfully romping together through the ecclesiastical woods did not appeal to the authorities and they did much to prevent it.

This ecclesiastical reticence did not help the morale of the clergy who took the possibility of joyful, Christian reunion seriously. During the 1960s, parallel with the delicate searching out by ecumenists of each other, the old style Protestant religious and political resistance to Catholics and Catholicism was being led more and more assuredly by Paisley who had now taken his place as the most recent and successful in a long line of anti-Catholic local preachers. He had enormous success not only in the streets but also in the normal church congregations. Many Protestant clergymen, even moderators of the Presbyterian Assembly, were afraid to oppose him because, they said, there was a danger of congregations leaving them for Paisley. We had occasion to remember rather sadly in those days the words of Jesus when some people refused to stay with him because his teaching was difficult to accept. He let them go.

Moderate and open-minded clergymen failed to confront the bitter inter-Christian rivalry which still existed in Northern Ireland or even construct a solid front against it. The strength of inter-Christian rivalries freshly stirred up most successfully by Paisley and the weakness of other Christian leaders weakened an already weak reconciling movement between Catholics and Protestant, Unionists and Nationalists.

Catholic churchmen were pre-occupied by the need to conform

to the policies of the Roman authorities, whatever their own assessment of local needs might be. The Roman authorities were carefully building up relationships with the Anglican church in Britain in the hope of eventual institutional agreement and even unity. At the same time Vatican foreign policy was to help create a strong, anti-Communist European alliance in which the Vatican itself would have considerable influence. To espouse the cause of 600,000 Roman Catholics in the North of Ireland whose interests were so obviously at variance with those of Britain, or the Anglican church, was not likely to be even a possible choice for the Vatican. During the 1960s and 1970s scarcely a word was issued from the Vatican which would be of any help to the Catholics in the North of Ireland either for their own morale or for their efforts at local reconciliation. It seemed that the prayer of Protestants in the North of Ireland that there should be no Pope there had been in effect answered. Catholic churchmen, deferential towards their Roman authorities, did not insist upon a local assessment of their problems being paramount. Protestant churchmen, haunted by the fact of dwindling congregations and the fear of losing much of what was left to Paisley, were afraid to go too far along the road to reconciliation even if they thought it was broadly speaking the right one.

In time, the open-minded clergy who had been elected moderators of the Presbyterian Assembly were replaced by others of a different stamp. By 1985 the moderatorship of the Presbyterian Church in Ireland was once again firmly in the hands of the strictly orthodox and ecumenically conservative. The whole process of liberalisation, followed by contestation and return to the ecclesiastical bunkers, had lasted about twenty years.

The work of open and ecumenical Protestant clergymen in the North was made more difficult of course by the rise of the Civil Rights movement in the late 1960s and the political pressure against change which was mounted at the same time. Two things might perhaps have helped the open-minded Protestant clergymen to weather the storm and to persuade others that ecumenism, open-mindedness and a new deal were worthwhile: an adequate theology which would have shown how to justify open-mindedness by an appeal to Christian truth, and some significant gestures made by Catholic church leaders which would have convinced them and their doubting friends that their efforts were succeeding. But the theology was not there and the gestures were not made.

There is, surprisingly, not a single instance on record during the years 1960 to 1985 which could be described as a generous gesture made by one church to another.

By 1984, then, in the North of Ireland strong political Protestantism had taken control of most of political life. One major party, the Democratic Unionist Party was founded and controlled by Protestant clergy, the other, the Official Unionist Party, was strongly influenced by Protestant clergymen through the Orange Order. Leadership in the Presbyterian Assembly had passed to the non-ecumenists who were deeply suspicious of Catholics and unwilling to make strong efforts to soften the bitter religious hatred which had disfigured so much inter-Christian life in Northern Ireland. Open-minded and generous clergymen had been in many cases forced to leave Northern Ireland to work elsewhere.

The case of the Rev. Armstrong of Limavady, who was forced to leave for Oxford, was only one of a long series of similar events, although it was treated by the press in Ireland as though it were a unique event. A prominent Protestant clergyman in Belfast from the mid-60s onwards kept a list of exiled clergymen pinned on his wall. As time went on the list became longer and included the names of the clergymen and their supposed faults. In one case it was, 'Prayed with Catholics', or 'Worshipped with Catholics'. I am not sure whether it included 'Prayed for Catholics' but it might well have done.

The number of displaced clergymen who had to go because of their work for greater open-mindedness and generosity among the Christians was large and depressing. Those who were able to stay often kept their thoughts to themselves. They were not helped towards great openness by the fact that eventually the Catholic church showed greater and greater signs of a return to authoritarian methods of dealing with its own people – Leonardo Boff disciplined in 1985 was also one of many – or by the fact that the Christians seemed unable to find any answers to many pressing social and moral problems except to argue about them. Clergymen began to realise, certainly at the beginning of the 1980s, that certain hidden and unthought-of problems observed by a few as early as the mid-1950s were beginning to catch up

with them: church attendance of about 5% to 15% for Protestants
and 25% to 40% for Catholics in a number of urban areas. What
it was in the North of Ireland as a whole was anybody's guess but
that it was too small and becoming smaller could not be doubted.
Ecumenism was far from Christian minds as they struggled with
the problem also of the diminishing seriousness with which they
were taken in the conduct of people's affairs. One day ecumenism
might indeed become necessary if only as a way of uniting
Christian forces against irrelevancy, but for the moment the
ecumenist, however much he might gain those things which God
loves, might well lose the things by which mere humans judged
him, large congregations, a healthy financial state and no
embarrassing encounters with the Paisleyites.

Many of the inter-Christian friendships which had been created
during this movement of reconciliation survived, but friendship
as such did not have a substantial effect on the thinking of
Christians as a whole. Some Christians were simply disappointed
that a respectful exchange of ideas had not produced a dramatic
result. Believing as some of them did that inter-Christian
antagonism was based on false information about each other, it
could only be disappointing to find that Christians distrusted each
other not only because they did not know but also because they
knew only too well what each was saying, doing and thinking. The
problem with the Christians as with the politicians was that in the
end one had not only to explain lovingly what one was thinking
but also to start thinking something else as well. Fresh religious
thinking was not likely, neither was fresh political thinking.
Radical religious or political thinking was not possible, except
among small groups who had little public influence.

On the one hand, worship was shared, and the Eucharist too,
in small groups who did what they did quietly; and on the other,
radical political ideas were inquired into by small groups of
Loyalists or Republicans. Those who knew where to go could
enjoy the stimulation of radical ideas among, as it were,
consenting adults; but the established political parties and
respectable churches were not the places in which they would
normally find themselves. If they were lucky they would perhaps
arrive at informal discussions between Loyalists and Republicans,
Catholics and Protestants, the kind of thing that could be
arranged, with more or less success at any time. The problem was

that what was being talked about was too often unacceptable to the religious and political leadership or to the public at large.

So political events, lack of courage, the strength of opposition to new ideas, all these made changes in Christian thinking in Northern Ireland difficult to achieve. It is easy to attribute this to tribalism but to do that is unworthy of the people in the North. Policies pursued by most churchmen were based on what they thought of as sound theological foundations. Regulation of inter-Christian marriages, of education, of social customs, of worship, all resulted from deeply felt religious needs. Friendship alone could never dissolve such restrictiveness or oppressiveness as resulted; what was needed was a generous and exciting restatement of Christian theology, a restatement for which neither the desire, courage nor competence existed. Those who ignored the restrictions imposed on worship sharing, on marriage or education soon found themselves exposed in an authoritarian society where the exposed member is too often left to survive by his or her own devices. The 'conservative' Christians needed a 'conservative' theology to back up what they did. They had it. The 'progressives' needed a 'progressive' theology to back up what they did. They had none.

There is a parallel here with what was happening in Northern Ireland politics. In politics no political thinking, no political theory or policy existed to match the generosity which many people in the North instinctively knew should be brought to bear on their political life. Radical people who took to the streets of Derry in 1968 realised that without a political philosophy they did it largely in vain, as one of them, Eamon McCann, has pointed out. The efforts, sometimes feeble, sometimes strong, which individual politicians made from time to time towards a new deal did not have a political philosophy which could be presented to their public. Terence O'Neill meeting Seán Lemass could not be justified by any political idea which had been presented to the Unionist population up to that point. Indeed it went against the only political theory they had ever heard – separation to the last inch. Without an adequate philosophy – or theology – the only initiatives likely to succeed are violent ones aimed against change.

The people who made the efforts were not necessarily the ones to blame. The intellectuals, however, could be blamed because they had been for all practical political and religious purposes dormant for many years, contributing almost nothing to any new ideas likely to emerge. Among Catholics, comment on what was said to be their most significant religious event for generations, the Second Vatican Council, was at best muted, at worst, ignorant. Political discussion among the intellectuals in the North from the 1950s to the 1980s was banal.

Some new thinking did emerge, some exciting changes of position among Republicans and Loyalists; some ecumenical people did share their Eucharist. The creation of new ideas for a new deal would have required, perhaps, some kind of demilitarised De Gaulle; or perhaps a John XXIII without his Vatican Council. Until some such paragon appeared no one seemed able to remove the stranglehold of religious and political institutions which had been created out of an old ideology and so were completely unable to create a new one.

9

A Christian Future?

When one says that Northern Ireland is a failed state or that it suffers from intractable problems, and apparently intractable people, we have to remind ourselves again and again that what we are talking about is one part of an experiment to create Christian states on Catholic and Protestant lines. Christian churchmen, North and South, who had considerable control of either education or politics or both proved incapable of bringing about humane change. Indeed they often opposed change when it was proposed by others; good will and intelligence were paralysed in a world created with the help of Christian religious and political ideals.

Because it seemed unlikely that fresh religious or political thinking would come from within Ireland, some people began to look to other countries for inspiration and help. But Christians in Northern Ireland in general tended to discourage involvement in their affairs by Christians in other countries. A convention existed, remarkably like the political convention which prevented interference by Westminster politicians, that Christians from abroad did not interfere religiously unless invited to do so by Irish clergymen. Such an invitation, as in the case of invitations to Westminster, was seldom given and sometimes Christians who wanted to be involved in Northern Ireland were discouraged. Mother Teresa's sisters were one of a number of examples, the only one publicised. Mother Teresa's sisters came to Belfast in 1972 and left unexpectedly in 1975. Their departure was due to the unwillingness of senior churchmen to have them there. Although she insisted that the decision to leave was hers alone, she really had no alternative. If she could not establish good working relationships with senior clergymen, and she could not, then there was no use continuing. As she remarked herself, there were many places in the world where people wanted the sisters, it was pointless staying where they did not. People in the district where they worked in Belfast were deeply saddened by their departure and regretted it deeply. Other Christians also were quietly made to abandon their plans of living in Belfast, or Northern Ireland, by fellow Christians.

Over the years a stream of missionaries had left Ireland for foreign countries in some of which – in ecclesiastically confined spaces – new thinking was emerging about the meaning of Christian witness in the harsh realities of modern economic and political life. Many missionaries returned home frequently to Ireland, and yet the new radical thinking which was said to be current abroad seemed not to penetrate into Ireland to any notable extent. One reason may have been that missionaries who needed financial and moral support from Irish Christians could not afford to be too free with liberal ideas while at home. The support might diminish. The same argument had been used by Archbishop Fulton Sheen when he was challenged as to why in his successful religious television programmes he did not invite the people of the United States to face the enormous problems of racism and poverty which they had at home. He replied that a great deal of the financial and moral support for the church's work in South and Central America came from viewers in the United States and it would be damaging to close off this source of help.

Whatever the reason, and perhaps the idea that Ireland had no need of fresh thinking was another, fresh ideas about Christian witness abroad were not noticeably penetrating into Ireland. Among Protestants there was a great deal of mistrust about financial and moral support given to countries in the Third World on the grounds that this might well be used to help 'subversive' movements there. If the influence of fresh ideas from abroad is noticeable in spite of this it may well be as much because of media exposure of what is happening in countries abroad as because of the influence of returned missionaries. In any case any fresh ideas which do appear in Ireland or in countries abroad do not take the Catholic world by storm in whirlwind fashion. On the contrary, they are voiced tentatively, even fearfully, and are always in danger of being rebuffed by church authorities or by the Christian majority.

If Christians in Ireland are to create fresh ideas they will have to do it for themselves and in all probability suffer the consequences.

The failure of the Christian experiment in Northern Ireland may well mean that the notion of managing a state on strict Christian lines must be finally abandoned. It would seem from experiences in Israel and Muslim countries that running a state according to the ethos of any religious group must be abandoned. Most of the oppressions of which Christians in Ireland have direct and painful knowledge were created by Christians, not by atheistic Marxists or agnostics. That being so, the Christians as such cannot be assumed to be able to solve the problems of any nation. They may indeed become a problem themselves.

The evolving situation in Northern Ireland is now revealing how impoverished the British or Irish view of democracy really is and how far we have to go to take the next step towards creating a democracy which will be humane and modern. It is doubtful if the clergy, with their entrenched idea that unchangingness is a virtue, will have anything to contribute to the debate about what our future democracy should be like. That is the strongest reason why clerical political power should be dissolved and education put into the hands of those whose immediate concern it is, the parents, teachers, students and holders of the public purse, any of whom can, of course, elect to education management committees as many clerics or as few as they wish. Clerical political power has proved damaging for the church in the North and for the state as well. The problem for clergymen is that once people begin to question the right of clergymen to run politics as they do in the North, or to run schools, as they do North and South, they will probably begin to question why they should manage anything, marriages, places of worship, church finances for example. Once these questions arise, a sound theology is needed to give reason for keeping things as they are or for necessary change. In the North we can see what inability to change has meant in both politics and religion.

Over all our problems in Ireland there hangs the shadow of a basic problem created and sustained by the British government. The government is a clericalist one and has learned through experience that it can favour the shepherds while fleecing the sheep. In Northern Ireland the British government has not been able to dissolve Catholic clergy control of schools by direct attack; to alienate the clergy would be an unacceptable risk. But it can and does humiliate the people, knowing that their support of the clergy will lessen opposition on the clergy's part to what they are doing to the people. If, however, the influence which the clergy have on people dissolves, there would be no compelling political reason why the clergy should be favoured any more; already there are signs that their influence is lessening, and, significantly, the government has now, against clerical protests, seriously reduced the control of Catholic churchmen over the training of teachers, amalgamating their colleges of education in Northern Ireland and reducing their staff. The favours granted to Catholic clergy, as in the past, are still proportionate to the need the British government feels of the clergy as a restraining influence on the people. Questioning the morality of the British regime in Ireland leads to the questioning of everything it does. This means that questions are bound to be asked some time about the nature of the churches' involvement in this or any state, about the military involvement of churches, about their teaching on industrial problems and many other things.

Church teaching on two matters in particular are bound to be thrown into question in the North; that of property and that of revolution. The Christian emphasis has traditionally been on the rights of those who own property but it is being pushed by some radical thinkers in the direction of protecting the rights of those who have none. Questioning this kind of teaching would lead to our looking at possible radical changes in the structure of our society. It would also help to provide an ideological link with those politicians who genuinely believe that policies must be made for and by the 'men of no property'.

The theology of a just revolution will also be questioned. The Christian churches do not have a duty to uphold any state although they often act as though they had; they have a duty to uphold whatever contributes to the dignity of human beings, and this may include the structures of the state or not. There is still a remnant within the churches of the belief that princes have a divine right to rule; the movement towards democracy which has occurred in political life has not been matched by a corresponding development of Christian theology. The rules for a moral or justified revolution are the same today as they were over a hundred and thirty years ago when Dr Murray of Maynooth lambasted those who foolishly believed that the common people could depose their rulers. Nowadays we know that the common people can depose their rulers not only for tyranny but for inefficiency and that it is the common people not the government itself who have the right to judge whether rulers are tyrannical or inefficient. The rules set out by the Christian churchmen about how and when a revolution can be justified have not changed to take account of new beliefs which the Christians themselves have accepted.

In Northern Ireland it is the commonly held Christian teaching that rulers who are in possession of government must be allowed to keep possession, that it is immoral to rebel against the government, and that Christian love can be practised in the community only after a firm framework of law and order has been imposed on it. This kind of teaching has made the task of unjust governments easy, because although the excesses of governments were challenged at least by those who suffered from them, the Christian basic teaching about government was never questioned by anybody. The divine rights of rulers and the primacy of law and order are concepts so sterile that Christians should suspect them at once.

Christian teachings about property and revolution have an obvious bearing on the situation in Northern Ireland; any challenge to that teaching would be a threat not only to the churches but to the support which churches give to the government. Churchmen are well aware of the risks involved in creating or allowing discussion about these matters. Yet, without putting it into theological terms people demand to know of what use is it to have the right to choose one's rulers if a government insists on denying one the use of that right; or if it refuses to acknowledge the rights of citizens to be heard through elected representatives of their choice. What use is it to have the rights of a person created, redeemed and inspired by God if we are told that we have no right to be heard and most disturbingly of all, if we have the right to choose our rulers and to replace them if they are not only tyrannical but inefficient, do we not also have a right to the means necessary to put that into effect? If a government which is tyrannical refuses to go, have we not the right to force it to go by whatever means are needed?

The questions are not posed in these terms, they are posed by every child with a stone in its hand aimed at a saracen, by every person who takes a gun and every woman who protests in a long line in a Belfast street against strip-searching. The church must give answers more relevant and democratic than those of Dr Murray of Maynooth in 1857.

I have made no secret of my own view, a view much changed from what I believed in 1965. The British government has oppressed and degraded our people, set them at each other's throats, offered the Protestants of Northern Ireland small gifts and the Catholics kicks, but by doing these things controlled them both. It has been an unjust regime and if it ceased to be so it would cease to rule. It has brought the Protestants into disgrace and forced many good citizens to come to the conclusion that only by the gun can they bring sense into their kind of politics.

I also believe that war is the worst of all ways to have to solve problems, but that if good people go to war we have to ask why it is that good people do such things. We must not accept that they are simply mindless killers because the government says they are. More and more I have come to believe that we must hold in honourable doubt what governments say. They have told untruths too often. They have told many untruths about Irish people and will be allowed to do so as long as Irish people think that British institutions are superior to their own and, therefore, hanker after some kind of British approval before they can believe that what they do or think or say has any merit. The institutions are not better and we as a free people need no validation from others. We need their friendship, their co-operation, but not their validation.

Therefore, we need to make our own assessment of our own situation using the same tools of analysis as we would use to discuss the affairs of France or Italy, or Nicaragua.

The Forum for a New Ireland promised to be the place where rational discussion could take place. But it was flawed at once by the declaration that only those would be heard who had given up 'violence', or military force for political purposes. This would have excluded so many parties and persons that the whole exercise should have become impossible there and then. But it did not become impossible because by common consent the exclusion meant only that Sinn Féin could not be heard. Yet members of that party were among the people's elected representatives.

This meant that the elected representatives of the constituency in which I live would not be heard. My neighbours would not be heard, although they live in an area which has been insistently and sorely abused by the British government.

No one in my district would be heard.

That is why I wrote a submission to the Forum for a New Ireland myself. I was not a representative of anyone, so I did not have the status of an elected representative as my justification for doing it.

I only had my anger.

10

Submission to the
New Ireland Forum

Lasting peace and stability in Ireland cannot be achieved unless the British government makes clear its reasons for remaining in Ireland and reveals its future plans regarding the North. To date, it has failed to do either of these things; progress towards peace by democratic means is, therefore, hindered or perhaps made impossible. In 1969, the British government stated that its commitment of troops was to protect Catholics, or to prevent Catholics and Protestants from becoming embroiled in street conflict. In later years the stated pupose was the defeat of the IRA. Later still the purpose was declared to be the defeat of international terrorism. The stated objective, then, varied according to the British government's need to explain its actions in terms most acceptable to international public opinion at any given time. Harold Wilson and Humphrey Atkins both admitted publicly that the commitment of troops in 1969 was to save the existing government from collapse. It is important to establish which of these explanations is true, or if any of them is true. The British government never explained in unequivocal terms the rationale behind its continuing presence in Ireland, and this means that all British initiatives in Northern Ireland must be suspect. They can be viewed as nothing more than holding operations which divert attention from real issues and, therefore, militate against ever finding a solution to the Northern Ireland problem. It is also highly doubtful if attempts to create democratic solutions will succeed, as if it is in the British government's interest to oppose and frustrate such solutions, it will not hesitate to do so. Significantly, any British initiative in terms of finding a solution, concerns itself only with coming up with solutions proposed by the British government and never by those most involved – the Irish citizens. Possible solutions (United Ireland, Federal Ireland, Independent Ulster, integration with the United Kingdom, return of the Stormont form of government) proposed by sections of the people are never on the table for discussion. In fact, the only solution which appears on the table for discussion is that proposed by the British government but unwanted by everyone else. Therefore, while the British government protests that it wants the people of Northern Ireland to come together to find a solution, what it really wants is that the people of Northern Ireland come together only to render workable suitable variants of the British government's solution. And, should the British government, for example, propose and set in motion a moderately democratic solution, powerful forces exist within the British system ready to thwart such a solution. In 1974 the British army had the men, the expertise and the firepower quite easily to control the events in Northern Ireland. A comparatively small number of Loyalists, badly organised and heavily infiltrated by the British forces, are said to have broken the Executive – the British government which had the force necessary to impose direct rule from London, maintained that it was powerless in the face of a Loyalist workers' strike – when what was in question was a new and more democratic form of government than that hitherto available from either Stormont or from London.

Whilst the British government's intentions are not clearly stated and whilst the British army is the strongest force in Northern Ireland it is not possible to negotiate peace. A clear and public statement of the British government's real aims, and the removal of the British army from the scene is essential if any progress is to be made. It is difficult to envisage how this can be achieved by democratic process, and, in the final analysis, it will probably be necessary to exercise some form of force on the British government. If we are to avoid the continual application of force by guerrilla armies (with the corruption of all our institutions as the British government reacts to it) we need to create increased diplomatic pressure and the pressure of public opinion. Indeed, it would seem reasonable to ask all parties in Ireland who recognise the damage perpetuated by the British regime in Northern Ireland, to examine all possible sanctions that can be applied. If this is not done then the situation can only deteriorate.

A solution must be found which will enable Protestant people to take their place in a new Irish democracy. But the realities of their position have to be faced. There are Protestants in Northern Ireland who want a new settlement, but they seem to be few and they are voiceless. They are an unrepresented minority in Ireland. Some Presbyterians still hold on to a liberal tradition and even some members of the Church of Ireland would be willing to see a new settlement in which they would be integrated into a new democracy. Such people are not, however, adequately represented either in political parties or in the leadership of their churches. Business people in Northern Ireland are realists and will go where the money is, whether they are Catholics or Protestants. If prosperity is available in a new democracy in Ireland, they will eventually consent to become part of that democracy. Already links are being forged between business people in the North and the South. External bank accounts along the Border areas – some of which are in the Gaelic version of names of Northern businessmen – are a symbol of the expediency which always wins over principle where money is involved. The discussion about the future of Ireland, therefore, should be primarily about economics, and about the impossibility of creating a good economy either North or South as long as the British government is in possession of a significant part of our resources, or whilst a significant part of our resources is involved in keeping the British government in possession.

It is important to remember, however, that in Northern Ireland political opinion among Protestants is led by clergy not by business people. This means that discussion of our situation often lacks practical and economic reality. Unless the clerical domination of Northern politics is dissolved, no rational economic argument can be brought to bear on the situation. The clergy have ensured that political discussion is unreal – that it does not deal with the economic and political realities of the modern world. It is unrealistic to ask Unionist/Protestant people in the North to consent to radical change. For many years after the two states were created in Ireland, the Protestants in the South did not give allegiance to the twenty-six County state. Their allegiance, as shown in their churches and lodges, was to the British state. The singing of the British national anthem in private and in church gatherings continued into the 1950s: discrimination in employment could be seen from advertisements and from the experiences of people seeking work. Such people would submit to a new regime but would not be loyal to it. Even today thousands of Protestants parade annually especially in Border areas, to demonstrate their loyalty to the British state. Such demonstrations are not just quaint survivals of old rituals, but rather a positive demonstration that loyalty to a state in which they live is still almost non-existent.

There cannot, then, be any firm prediction that Protestants in Ireland will be loyal to any new emerging state no matter how democratic, if they have not complete control of its institutions. However sombre such a thought may be, it has to be entertained in view of past experience and in view of repeated refusals of Protestant church and political leaders to countenance any advance towards a democracy for all the thirty-two counties of Ireland. Whatever arrangement is made, we can reasonably expect that Protestants, with the exception of those few who recognise the benefits of radical change, will withhold their loyalty from any new political structures which they do not totally control. This is a reality with which Irish people must learn to live, and which they must take into account when discussion of possible future structures begins. It is discouraging, but it must not be allowed to hinder forever the creation of democratic structures in Ireland. Again and again, we return to the unhappy necessity of using force to achieve just and democratic government. The question of what form the force must take has to be honestly faced. We need a solution to this problem which will be both humane and successful.

Meanwhile, although much of our discussion is about ensuring that the rights of Protestants are respected, the Protestant minority in Ireland is extremely well-organised, well-respected, well-protected and well-armed. The fact that members of the Protestant clergy in the North are in certain areas members also of the British armed forces is a symbol of the extent to which being armed is part of the Northern Protestant way of life. How many Protestants have arms or have access to arms is impossible to say, but the policy of successive British governments has been to arm Protestants whilst disarming Catholics. The end result is that in Northern Ireland we have the best armed and best officially protected minority in Europe – the Protestants; any proposed solution has to take this into account.

The Forum must also honestly face what it is asking when it invites only those who have renounced violence to take part in discussions. Neither the British Conservative Party nor the British Labour Party have renounced violence. And to admit the DUP to discussions reserved solely for those who have renounced violence is clearly ludicrous. The entire world must bear witness to the violence of the state constructed by the Unionist Party. British policies in Ireland have always been, and are, violent. Admission to discussion only of those who reject violence then would automatically mean rejection of both major British political parties, the DUP, and the Official Unionists. Therefore, what the Forum really means is that it rejects Sinn Féin and, if this is what it means, it should have said so openly and honestly. The general public would have understood the position, just as it understands the acceptance of the Paisleyites on Radio Telefís Éireann and the rejection of Sinn Féin as an illogicality brought about by political expediency. It is a foolish, untenable position that must be reconsidered. All interested parties must be admitted to discussion. All parties who can influence the situation in the North must also be admitted to discussion. Otherwise, no political progress can be made and people will be sacrificed to pseudo-morality. To reject from discussion those who condone violence would be to reject from discussion one of the principal parties, the British government.

Whether political parties or churches like it or not, Sinn Féin has been deliberately voted for by a large number of people. No one can plead the democratic process while rejecting the representatives chosen by the people. To begin discussion of democratic processes by rejecting those whom so many people have chosen to represent them is both unrealistic and undemocratic. The excuse given for listening to Paisley (that although he is violent he represents the views of many people and has been voted for as their representative) is not allowed to influence the rejection of Sinn Féin. Rejection of Sinn Féin is an arrogant rejection of the choice of many people and will be seen as such by those who elected them; it will not appease elements in the DUP or the OUP. Whether Sinn Féin choose to enter into discussions with the Forum or not is something which they would, in time, have to answer for to their own voters.

The Forum, in common with Unionist parties and the British

government, has said to people: 'Unless you elect representatives of whom we approve we shall not talk to you.' Refusing to talk to elected representatives is tantamount to refusing to talk to people who suffer most from the situation the Forum is trying to remedy. All protestations about the democratic process are invalidated by such a decision on the part of the Forum. The decision marginalises for example, the people of West Belfast, whose main political grievance is precisely this, that those in positions of power and authority have refused to listen to them and that they cannot enter the democratic process except by adhering to parties chosen not *by* them but *for* them by others.

It must be said, unequivocally, that the Unionist and British establishment in Northern Ireland have lost any right they may have had to rule in Ireland. Their persistent and absolute refusal to admit a large number of their fellow citizens to any effective part in the government of their own country means that injustice and bad government are built into the only system of government which they are willing or able to create in Ireland. That being so, they have no right to rule.

Their tenure of government has as its moral basis only the fact that they are in possesssion. The principle that a bad government is better than no government at all is the sole moral principle on which the tenure of the British government and that of the Unionist government in Ireland rests. The absolute refusal of the Unionists to share power, resources and government with Catholics must be recognised, as must the fact that their refusal does not depend on the refusal of Catholics to co-operate in government. From time to time this has been tested, for example, by Catholics becoming an opposition party in parliament, even by Catholics such as the late J. J. Campbell and others offering to become members of the only party allowed to govern. Those offers were refused in absolute terms.

There was never any question of the decision to allow Catholics to take part in government being conditional on their changing their political or religious views. Even that would not suffice to earn a place in government. What was in question was not acceptance of British rule – these people accepted it – but the fact that they belonged to a religious group which was unacceptable. The refusal of the Unionists, who represent about 60% of the population, and particularly of the Paisleyites who probably represent about 40% of the Protestants voters, to share power in even the most rudimentary way is absolute. This means, in effect, that an internal just and reasonable solution to the Northern Ireland problem is impossible; not because of 'subversives' or because of abnormal politics but because normal politics in Northern Ireland must require absolute refusal of a just share in political processes. There is no way out of this impasse except by some kind of force. Absolute refusal to allow Catholics to take part in government in matters which concern them and for which they pay taxes will not and cannot be revised in the light of some future acceptance by Catholics of the British state. This has been stated by Unionist and Protestant leaders many times and they have made it clear that it is not up for discussion.

A party or government which excludes over 40% of a population in this way is acting immorally and has no right to rule; its rule is tolerated because it is in power, and resented because it remains in power by force. The depth of unwillingness of Protestants at all levels to allow Catholics to make political choices was seen in the strong reaction to the Catholic vote of about 43% for Sinn Féin. This was declared a moral evil. Almost exactly the same proportion of Protestants voters voted for Paisley, without adverse comment from churchmen and politicians. The difference between the two votes is not that one is for violence and the other is not; it is that one is for giving political power to all citizens and the other is not. Paisley and Unionist policy is to exclude over 40% of electors from power; Sinn Féin stated policy is to include them. The Forum cannot honestly point to what it sees as immorality in one place and refuse to recognise it in another. Some moral principles have to be stated in political discussion and the realities of politics have to be faced, even if it means reaching unwelcome conclusions. Since neither Unionists nor the British government have the right to impose unjust rule, force of some kind must be used. A major question facing the Forum then is the nature of such force.

As already pointed out, the British army has on two occasions, 1914 and 1974, made itself unavailable to its own government to carry out its will in Ireland. Could it be that the same thing occurred on Bloody Sunday? There is, then, a strong political argument for the removal of the British army during any period which calls for force or when negotiations have to be entered into.

There must be no doubt in people's minds as to the real reasons why the British army cannot be trusted. Distrust is based on solid historical and political reasons and experience. Any solution to the North of Ireland problems, especially a liberal and reasonable solution, would be endangered and perhaps destoyed by the refusal of the British army to carry out the will of its own government. As the British army is less available to a Labour government then to a Conservative one, the Conservative government is at least marginally more capable of acquiring a back-up force in the North of Ireland.

Serious constitutional questions regarding freedom of action face British governments, but these are British problems which the British have to solve – and Irish people should never be obliged to suffer because of internal British constitutional problems.

Our position in this matter has been misrepresented and we in Ireland have been made to appear foolishly idealistic, our dislike of the British army being based on petty nationalism or experienced brutalities. It is, on the contrary, a question of political possibilities of reasonable trust. If there is an element in our situation which makes a solution to it impossible or extremely difficult it must be honestly faced and dealt with. The British army is not part of the solution in any sense. It always has been and probably, because of the structure of power in Britain, always will be, a substantial part of the problem and a formidable barrier against a solution. Those who have decided that military means must be used against the British government to remove the British army from the North of Ireland have recognised this. Those who reject the use of military means to solve the problem must accept that the British army must be removed by strong diplomacy and negotiation, by educating the public about the true nature of the British army's function in Northern Ireland and its probable unwillingness to provide the back-up necessary for a negotiated settlement.

The fact that clergy play so large a part in politics in Northern Ireland is a major problem because it is very difficult, perhaps impossible, to introduce or sustain any rational argument based on economics or normal politics. The clerical dominance of politics has to be dissolved before reasonable political dialogue can take place. Once a political change occurs, clergy traditionally assent to new institutions, that is to say, although they may not be loyal to them, they will not as a rule foment revolution against them. The clergy in general are a powerful force against change. Once a significant political change has occurred, they fulfil their role by reinforcing the new state of affairs, provided they can build their power within it. It can be assumed that this will happen in Ireland. If significant change is to occur, clerical dominance of politics in Northern Ireland must be challenged. This is one of the most difficult and necessary tasks we face.

If any strong political party emerges which is clerically dominated or clerically supported – on any side – this will create further difficulties. The task is not to create a clerically supported party on the Nationalist side to balance the clerically dominated Unionist and British parties in the conflict, but to dissolve the clerical domination. Catholic politicians have made more progress in counteracting clerical domination than their Protestant counterparts. The fear of offending the clergy is still a potent factor among Protestant journalists and others in Northern Ireland. There is good reason for this: we have allowed preoccupation with clerical influence in the South to blind us to the reality of extreme clerical control of politics in the North. Change will be prevented if possible, but this does not mean that once it takes place, clerics will rebel against it militarily. Dissolving clerical domination poses a serious problem, but whatever the solution, the problem must be stated and faced. Otherwise, there is no possibility of solving the problems of Northern Ireland. If, on the other hand, people can see that such a problem exists in the North then the Unionist argument against the clerical element in the South is weakened.

In general, the British interpretation of events in Ireland has been accepted by both politicians and churchmen and the Irish government itself. It has also been accepted abroad, particularly in the United States. People accept the British definition of terrorism. They accept the definition of the problem in Northern Ireland as one of disagreement between Catholics and Protestants with a benign British government standing democratically between them. All definitions and descriptions of the Northern Ireland situation must be challenged, because they are at the root of much misunderstanding of the problems. It is impossible to enlist the help of friends in foreign countries as long as they are persuaded that the British description of Irish situations is a correct one, and as long as people accept the British description of Irish democrats as 'irrational'. Unfortunately, this kind of interpretation and description of problems in Ireland has been allowed to pass unchallenged by successive Irish governments and has been reinforced by churchmen and other groups. The result of this is that British government information services abroad have an easy task. People in other countries have never been told about the true nature of the Irish state and that of the British state. They have never been invited to consider whether the Irish Constitution or the British political system is the better expression of modern democracy – within the British system a House of unelected Lords, a state church, a powerful monarchy with hereditary succession and ill-defined powers – within the Irish system rejection of the State Church, a confessional state and unelected lawmakers. People in foreign countries are allowed to believe that Irish democrats are fighting against or arguing against or refusing to live under the world's most developed democracy, when what is in question is the refusal of Irish democrats to countenance any efforts to perpetuate a medieval aristocratic system in Ireland. A potentially significant case that the Irish Constitution, even as it stands, represents the more advanced democracy of the two has gone by default. Instead, our arguments have been weakened by the reiteration by prominent Irish speakers and writers of the defects of the Irish system. It comes as a surprise then to people in other countries to learn that Ireland has a modern, liberal democratic Constitution while the British have a monarchical, aristocratic system which is one of the most archaic in Europe. Posed in terms such as these, the Irish case to be allowed to construct a democracy for itself is at once seen to be rational and based on sound modern democratic principles. A new and fresh presentation of the Irish case, the demand to be allowed to construct a modern democracy in Ireland, is required. It has, in a real sense, little to do with the evils of the past. It has everything to do with the future of democracy in Ireland and, indeed, in Europe. In any contest between an archaic aristocratic system which cannot be substantially reformed and a young, vigorous democratic state struggling to develop its potential, the young democracy is bound to win. It is in terms like these rather than in terms of ancient Ireland sighing under a foreign yoke that the case must be presented. But the case must be presented in a way that is vigorous and initially uncompromising. Either Irish democrats will claim what is theirs by right or they will not. If they will not, then let the Forum dissolve and let the appalling regime in the North of Ireland continue. But if we want a democracy in Ireland, we have to make it crystal clear that we are going to struggle for it with every means at our disposal.

It has often been said that people in the Republic of Ireland have to think first of the survival of their own economy and, therefore, the problem of the North has to be temporarily ignored. But it could just as strongly be argued that the Irish economy can neither develop nor survive until the Northern problem is solved. Therefore, solving the Northern problem is tantamount to providing a solution to the economic future of the thirty-two counties of Ireland. The waste of resources sustaining the present regime in the North is disastrous. The failure of Irish people to unite to use all their resources for economic development is ill-advised. It can also be strongly argued that the partition of Ireland had more to do with the British need for bases and its desire to prevent the emergence of a viable Irish economy than it had to do with the protection of Irish Protestants. The Irish economy cannot develop adequately unless the Northern problem is solved; it is a fallacy to argue that the Republic must solve its own economic problems before addressing itself to the problems of the North. The Northern problem is very largely an Irish economic problem.

It has also been suggested that the interest of Protestants is a primary motive for British policy in the North of Ireland. Yet British policy in Ireland has brought shame, fear and a measure of disgrace to Irish Protestants. It has to be clearly stated that British policy either was not directed to the protection of Protestants or that it failed miserably and, therefore, must be supplanted. It must also be clearly stated that Irish Protestants cannot depend on Britain for protection; they must protect themselves, but they can only do so in company with their fellow Irish citizens whatever their faith. It is only in this context that discussion of guarantees becomes significant. But the argument must be made that British intentions are always suspect. In view of the treatment of people in Northern Ireland at the hands of the British government, the description of the British as a friendly nation is surely ludicrous. The resolution of the present situation in Northern Ireland calls for firmness as well as friendship. There must be an end to any attempt to build new relationships based on false interpretations of what we are or what we do. If the British government wishes to take a useful step forward it could well put all the choices made by significant sections of the Irish people on the table for discussion. To date this has not been done. That Britain has been allowed, over so many years, to refuse this simple gesture is a symbol of the weakness we show in face of foreign force.

11

An Honourable Settlement?

It is likely that the British government could not grant any kind of democracy in Northern Ireland without causing an acute constitutional crisis in Britain. But if they were forced to make some kind of agreement with the Irish government and the political parties in the North, what are the chances of such an agreement being useful to Irish people and being kept by the British? Our experience with the Sunningdale agreement (1973) leading to the Northern Ireland power-sharing executive must make us pessimistic on both counts. The British government having made the agreement in 1973 did not enforce it in 1974.

But the most serious aspect of that affair from the Irish point of view is that while the British did not carry out their obligations under the agreement, the Irish government kept theirs. Sunningdale is the latest in a long, sad series of agreements which the British have broken.

By the Sunningdale agreement of 1973 the Irish government undertook to ensure that people who committed offences in one jurisdiction could be tried in the other – which was done. It promised to facilitate extradition – this was done. It promised to bring its laws into the line with European Convention standards – this was actively promoted. It promised to set up a police authority – this was actively pursued. It promised to set up an independent police complaints authority – this is being actively pursued.

On the other side, the British government promised to facilitate the setting up of a Council of Ireland and a power-sharing executive in Northern Ireland – it failed to do either of these things effectively, the excuse being that the Loyalists had prevented them. They promised to put an end to internment – they did not do so, but instead continued internment by other means, for example, long remands of up to three years, the equivalent of a six year sentence. Because a number of British government promises were dependent upon the creation of a Council of Ireland and a power-sharing executive in the North, the failure to set up these meant that Britain was able to renege on almost all its obligations as a result. In general the British government got all it asked for, extradition, trial of prisoners in the Republic for offences committed elsewhere, agreement in principle on measures which would benefit both countries but Britain chiefly as the larger and more powerful partner. When the British government allowed the Council of Ireland to be reneged upon and the power-sharing executive to fall, its obligations fell away. Within six months the British obligations under the Sunningdale agreement had melted away like snow off a ditch. On the Irish side, what the Irish government could not deliver at once it worked so hard on that by 1985 it was still doing the best it could to satisfy British demands. It was a self sacrificing attitude on the part of an Irish government whose people were getting nothing in return. Unfortunately it was really the dispossessed people in the North who were being sacrificed to what they could see being presented as a particularly revolting form of government righteousness. To be sacrificed to righteousness might have some compensations; to be sacrificed to incompetence had none.

The British government claimed that the reason why it reneged on its obligations was that Northern Loyalists refused to allow the Council of Ireland. Loyalist objections were nearer home: they just refused to give any share of government whatsoever to Catholics. Since 1974 the refusal of Loyalists to allow the agreement to be put into effect has been the main topic of discussion about Sunningdale; there has been absolutely no discussion of the remarkable fact that while Irish obligations under an agreement not ratified by Dáil Éireann have been in the main fulfilled, British obligations have been entirely unfulfilled.

One could say that the Irish representatives at Sunningdale were simply incompetent and did not know what they were getting into. They must have been incompetent after Sunningdale, whatever about the process of making the agreement, otherwise they would not have allowed the British to behave the way they did. But there is a clear indication in the Sunningdale agreement communiqué of December 1973 that the Irish delegates did indeed know what they were about, and how careful they had to be about what was agreed. This indication is in paragraph five of the Sunningdale document.

Of the twenty paragraphs in the agreement the British and Irish delegates agreed on a formula for all except one. This was paragraph five. The two versions of this paragraph were given side by side, descriptive of the 'aspirations' of both parties:

Irish Version

The Irish government fully accepted and solemnly declared that there could be no change in the status of Northern Ireland until a majority of the people of Northern Ireland desired a change in that status.

British Version

The British government solemnly declared that it was, and would remain, its policy to support the wishes of the majority of the people of Northern Ireland. The present status of Northern Ireland is that it is part of the United Kingdom. If in the future, the majority of the people of Northern Ireland should indicate a wish to become part of a United Ireland, the British government would support that wish.

The differences between the two versions were extraordinary and very revealing. The Irish delegates were clearly aware of the implications of what the British were saying and how different it was from what they were saying. But for some equally extraordinary reason discussion about this in Ireland was muted and politicians and churchmen still talked about persuasion towards unity as the only practical policy. It was, we can gather from the wording of the British version of paragraph five, a futile policy.

What the Irish side was saying was that there should be no change in the status of Northern Ireland until a majority of the people there wanted it. The time was 1973 when a proportion of roughly 60% to 40% of the population of Northern Ireland was divided into the two traditional political camps. One can say that these were traditionally the proportions of people who would favour a united Ireland and those who would not. The analysis is a crude one and would have to be modified to give a true picture of political allegiances in the North of Ireland, but it is clear that a swing of 10% in the traditional 'Protestant' or Unionist camp would be extremely significant – a swing of even 5% would make the case for substantial political change unanswerable. It might seem that in the North of Ireland such a swing of opinion would be improbable. But it was 1973, when some Loyalists were beginning to question old loyalties, when there was the beginning of discussion about an Independent Northern Ireland. Sinn Féin had made the offer of a four state federation in which Ulster would have a fair measure of control over its own affairs. There were splits in the Unionists camps; the UDA had firmly rejected some of the old religious and political establishments. Even British officials had been prepared to admit that the morale of the troops was low. The functions of the RUC had been taken over by the military. The Stormont government had been dissolved. Protestants were rethinking their loyalties in a way that had not been evident for many years. Political leaders in Britain were at least thinking about possible withdrawal as a way of protecting their vital interests. The possibility of a significant swing of Protestant opinion in the direction of some change had to be taken into account. From the point of view of British interests it was important that the swing required to oust them completely should be so great as to be unpractical. If such a swing occurred, and an Irish government might consider it a duty to help it occur, than radical change would be on the way.

The British government side, however, had a very clear idea of what kind of majority would be needed for any change.

It did not say that if *a majority* in Northern Ireland wished to enter a United Ireland it would accede to this desire; it said that if *the majority* wished it, it would accede to it. For those living in the North of Ireland the difference between 'a majority' and 'the majority' was only too clear.

In the North of Ireland the term 'the majority' is a political technical term. It means the Protestant Unionist population. Catholics are referred to as 'the minority' by British politicians, Irish politicans and churchmen in spite of appeals made to them to stop doing so because the term is inaccurate, politically dangerous and morally degrading. Catholics are not simply *a* minority, they are *The* Minority; the Protestant Unionists are not simply *a* majority, they are *The* Majority (which will remain the decisive part of the population in face of even major shifts of political opinion).

What the British government says in paragraph five is that if the Protestant Unionist population wants to become part of a United Ireland the British government will facilitate that desire. Even in 1973, a time of changing opinions, it was a safe thing to say.

What the British and Irish government policy of unity by persuasion really means – as far as the British are concerned – is more than 50% of Protestants voting for it, not, needless to say, the Catholic 40% plus 10% of the Protestants. In the matter of constitutional arrangements in Northern Ireland, clearly, 50% of the Protestant vote must achieve what 100% of the Catholic vote can not.

Given the British determination to stay in Ireland, straight majority vote or no majority vote, it is not surprising that the British government could not accept the Irish version of paragraph five. And given the Irish view of the situation it was impossible for the Irish delegates to accept the British version. So they wrote two different versions each saying radically different things.

It is not surprising. What was surprising was the lack of discussion in Ireland about what the British government was saying; the continual reassertion of an Irish government policy of consent to unity when it is clear that such consent would have to be of more than 50% of the Northern Protestants, and the continuing belief that any agreement can be reached with the British government which would be advantageous to Irish people or honourably observed on the British side. The Sunningdale Agreement 1973 and its aftermath should serve as a valuable lesson to Irish politicians.

The advantage to the Irish government of allowing the British to act in the way they do is not at all clear. Perhaps they do it out of fear, or out of reverence for their old masters, or because they want to defeat the Republicans, or because they think it best for the Irish people. One possible advantage in not discussing the meaning of the Sunningdale Agreement could be simply than an Irish government can still present to the Irish public the idea that unity by consent is a practical and achievable goal. It is not

practical – but this is not because Unionists cannot be convinced,
perhaps they can, it is because even if they *were* convinced, the
British government would not for that reason grant them what
they wished for, if that should involve removal of the British
military and economic apparatus from Ireland.

The chances of any agreement being reached now or of any
such agreement being advantageous, or if advantageous being
honourably implemented by the British government are so remote
that no one need take   them seriously.

It is time to think of sanctions instead.

Meanwhile, one may well reflect on the men who signed the
Sunningdale Communiqué in December 1973: Edward Heath
who described himself as 'the best friend Ulster ever had'; Gerry
Fitt, now holder of a seat in the British House of Lords; Oliver
Napier, knighted by her Majesty Queen Elizabeth for services
rendered; Brian Faulkner, later member of the British House of
Lords, earlier responsible for introducing internment without
trial accompanied by torture; and Liam Mac Cosgair who
belonged to Fine Gael.

Bobby Sands and the Tragedy of Northern Ireland

John M. Feehan

Bobby Sands captured the imagination of the world when, despite predictions, he was elected a Member of Parliament to the British House of Commons while still on hunger-strike in the Northern Ireland concentration camp of Long Kesh.

— When he later died after sixty-six gruelling days of hunger he commanded more television, radio and newspaper coverage than the papal visits or royal weddings.

— What was the secret of this young man who set himself against the might of an empire and who became a microcosm of the whole Northern question and a moral catalyst for the Southern Irish conscience?

— In calm, restrained language John M. Feehan records the life of Bobby Sands with whom he had little sympathy at the beginning – though this was to change. At the same time he gives us an illuminating and crystal-clear account of the terrifying statelet of Northern Ireland today and of the fierce guerrilla warfare that is rapidly turning Northern Ireland into Britain's Vietnam.

One Day in My Life

Bobby Sands

One Day in My Life is a human document of suffering, determination, anguish, courage and faith. It also portrays frightening examples of man's inhumanity to man.

Written with economy and a dry humour it charts, almost minute by minute, a brave man's struggle to preserve his identity against cold, dirt and boredom. It is the record of a single day and conjures up vividly the enclosed hell of Long Kesh; the poor food, the harassment and the humiliating mirror searches. Bobby Sands and his comrades were often gripped by terror at the iron system that held them and yet their courage never faltered.

Written on toilet paper with a biro refill and hidden inside Bobby Sands' own body, this is a book about human bravery and endurance and will take its place beside the great European classics on imprisonment like *One Day in the Life of Ivan Denisovich* and our own John Mitchel's *Jail Journal*.

'I wish it were possible to ensure that those in charge of formulating British policy in Ireland would read these pages. They might begin to understand the deep injuries which British policy has inflicted upon this nation, and now seek to heal these wounds.' *From the Introduction by Seán MacBride.*

Bobby Sands was twenty-seven years old when he died, on the sixty-sixth day of his hunger strike, on 5 May 1981. He had spent almost the last nine years of his short life in prison because of his Irish Republican activities. By the time of his death he was world-famous for having embarrassed the British establishment by being elected as M.P. to the British Parliament for Fermanagh/South Tyrone and having defiantly withstood political and moral pressure to abandon his hunger-strike.

"Infertility is painful. In these pages, Matthew Arbo gives biblical insight and wise counsel, offering both comfort and hope for those on this difficult journey. *Walking through Infertility* goes deeper than the superficial clichés couples often hear, which, though intended to comfort, can hurt. Arbo frames infertility within the biblical narrative, where it is actually quite common and significant—we find we are not alone. Additionally, he helps those navigating some of the complex ethical decisions made possible by modern technology for dealing with infertility—we are not without guidance. Ultimately, he points to our comfort in the community of the church and our hope in the God of life."

Joshua Ryan Butler, Pastor, Imago Dei Community,
Portland, Oregon; author, *The Skeletons in God's Closet* and
The Pursuing God

"I am glad to commend Matthew Arbo's *Walking through Infertility* both to couples going down this road and to the friends, family members, and professionals who walk this road with them. It is sensitively done, and full of wisdom and insight about what these couples are facing. It's a worthwhile resource, which I will often consult."

Scott B. Rae, Professor of Christian Ethics, Talbot School of
Theology, Biola University

"*Walking through Infertility* is a resource I wish had been available when we walked through our own struggles with infertility. In an age of increasing medical advancement, the options for couples are numerous and often overwhelming. Matthew Arbo has provided a helpful resource for couples as they consider what the Bible has to say about infertility and how God's Word speaks to the various treatments out there. But Arbo also speaks to church leaders, who are often left wondering how to counsel those under their care. This is a needed book, and I'm glad it's finally here."

Courtney Reissig, author, *Glory in the Ordinary* and
The Accidental Feminist